Organic

Organic

Don Burke's Guide to Growing Organic Food

Inside

Introduction 6

What is organic? 17

Building and planting an organic vegetable garden 20
Construction and soil preparation 23
Preparing for planting 35
Spring planting 45
Making a scarecrow 63
Recipes from the garden 69
Autumn planting 85

Staying organic 100
Harvest and storage 103
Preserving 118
The art of compost 123
Pots, tubs and troughs 141
Kids in the garden 151
Keeping chooks 157

Real people who've done it themselves — **172**
Gardening in small spaces — 175
An organic country garden — 187

What to grow — **200**
A–Z of vegetables — 203
Heirloom vegetables — 239
The best backyard fruits — 247
Herbs — 269

Problem solving: pests and diseases — **278**
Safe pest control — 280
Friends and foes — 284
Companion planting — 297

Index — 299

Lift-out wall chart — **305**

RIGHT: 1962 – as a teenager I loved growing silver beet for my budgies.

FAR RIGHT: This is me identifying a poppy in Melbourne in 1949, aged two.

Introduction

As a six-year-old kid, I started my own vegie garden. On my own. I planted radishes and they grew up quickly. I can still remember the superb taste of my first crop and how proud I was when I took some inside and presented them to the family.

My 'Pa' Arthur Hyatt was a skilled vegetable gardener; 1917.

Soon after I started growing silver beet for my budgies as well as various other crops. When I went to stay with my grandparents during school holidays, I watched and helped my grandfather in his vegetable garden. He grew beans, peas, lettuce, tomatoes and dozens of other plants. Pa (as I called him) was a skilled vegetable gardener and the few precious weeks that I spent with him were a very special time for me.

The fresh vegies tasted so good. Picking them was so much fun.

The world of growing your own food is a deeply rewarding one. You can grow many varieties of heritage vegetables, some that date back over 100 years. These varieties

I hit a Floradade tomato up against a wall with a tennis racquet on the TV show *Burke's Backyard* in 1987. This was a horrible tomato that had been bred to last well on the supermarket shelves and look nice, but was absolutely flavourless. It survived several minutes of being bounced up against the wall.

are quite different to the ones available at fruit shops or supermarkets. Supermarkets demand varieties that have a long shelf life, so that they don't have to throw them out after a day or so. They need heavy-cropping plants that are easily harvested and therefore cheap.

The end result of all of this culminated in the tasteless tomatoes of the 1970s and 1980s. Floradade and similar varieties of tomatoes looked beautiful and lasted well on the shelves. But they didn't taste like tomatoes, so I grabbed a Floradade and a tennis racquet and hit it up against a brick wall for several minutes. This was 1987 and, as I did it on *Burke's Backyard* on television, I explained what a truly awful tomato it was. After several minutes of hitting, it was still unmarked.

The TV segment caused a furore amongst the public who demanded tastier tomatoes. The supermarkets responded by insisting on better varieties and the Floradade types crashed in popularity.

Over the longer term there was a revival of interest in heritage varieties of tomatoes and vegies in general. These old-fashioned varieties were almost extinct, but the odd source of seed here and there was found and many of the varieties were saved.

These heritage varieties and other modern home varieties of tomatoes and other fruit and vegetables really are a lot better. They do taste wonderful, but they also tend to crop over a much longer period. At home you don't want all of your tomatoes ripe at the same time, but as a commercial grower you do (for ease of harvesting). Home varieties crop over many weeks, feeding the family far better.

Equally, you don't need a house variety of vegie to last a long time once picked, as you will pick and eat them while they are fresh.

TOP LEFT: Green grape tomatoes.

TOP RIGHT: Various heirloom tomato varieties.

BOTTOM LEFT: Sapphire potatoes.

BOTTOM RIGHT: Rainbow chard.

New old varieties

Now you can get yellow, orange, black or even striped tomatoes. Some are shaped like pears (large or small), others like eggs. You can get purple-fleshed or yellow-fleshed potatoes, red, yellow or purple-stemmed silver beet and literally hundreds of other spectacular fruits and vegetables.

Perhaps the fun bit is sharing. When you produce a glut (and you will) you can give your excess fruit to family, friends and neighbours. More and more across Australia, neighbours are swapping fresh produce with each other. You grow superb tomatoes, eggplants and carrots, and you swap them with the lady up the road who grows great lettuces, beans and peas. This develops friendships and often forms the basis of small local communities, much like the way people used to live.

Equally, you can preserve, dry out, or freeze your excess produce, or turn it into jams. These too make excellent gifts or swap items for neighbours. Personalised items like this are perfect gifts for the person 'who has everything'.

Organic produce

When I was a kid, toxic chemicals were everywhere. Agricultural chemicals were still fairly new and everyone regarded them as wonderful new products that had saved the world.

Soldiers dusted themselves with DDT in the trenches. People used Chlordane and Dieldrin as common pesticides—especially for termite control.

Most gardeners used heaps of toxic sprays and I remember the media gardening expert of the 1950s, Alan Seale, telling me that using Maldison (the main garden pest spray) had caused his hair and fingernails to fall out. His hair regrew to some extent, but his fingernails remained quite damaged.

BELOW: 1945. Released Australian POWs having their clothes deloused using DDT at the Yokohama shipping docks, Japan, prior to being shipped home to Australia. *Australian War Memorial Negative Number 019285*

Rachel Carson wrote her seminal book *Silent Spring* in 1962, which exposed awful dangers in indiscriminate use of chemicals in the environment. This led to the beginnings of the popular environment movements around the world.

This in turn led to the eventual banning of the DDT family of chemicals in most areas around the world. Chemicals like DDT, Chlordane, Dieldrin, Heptachlor, Endrin and several others were eventually banned in Australia. Australia was rather slow to ban these chemicals partly because there was no national body which controlled chemicals and partly because environmentalists and gardening experts failed to act.

Eventually I contacted the Minister for Primary Industries at the time, Simon Crean, and together we established the (then) National Registration Authority for Agricultural and Veterinary Chemicals (NRAAVC). Once this was going, as a board member I pressed for the banning of these chemicals and the rest of the board supported me.

This body is now the Australian Pesticides and Veterinary Medicines Authority (APVMA). It has continued to remove the worst of the agricultural and veterinary chemicals and also to improve the usage of the remaining chemicals.

TOP LEFT. Dumpy, New Guinea. Natives employed by the 18th Australian Anti-malarial Control Unit operating rotary blowers full of DDT powder. *Australian War Memorial Negative Number 061441*

TOP RIGHT: 1946, Willoughby, Sydney. Re-drumming of DDT anti-insect spray from 46 gallon drums to 4 gallon drums at the 1st Supply Reserve Depot. *Australian War Memorial Negative Number 129142*

Organic fertilisers

These are still a problem. Basically, there are no effective regulations that guarantee that a fertiliser labelled 'organic' is truthfully labelled. So, many fertilisers labelled 'organic' do in fact contain artificial (inorganic) ingredients—they may even constitute the majority of the contents. When the NRAAVC was formed, the states passed on most regulatory issues to that body, but conveniently let the issue of labelling of organic fertilisers etc fall into oblivion.

In an effort to flag the problem, we tested blood and bone products on *Burke's Backyard*. We paid a private detective to purchase samples of all major brands of blood and bone. He then placed samples of each one into blank containers labelled A, B, C etc. These samples were sent to two scientific laboratories, of which one was the Australian Government Analytical Laboratories, and a third sample was sent to a major forensic laboratory to test for either blood or bone traces.

Many of the brands were impure and one contained no blood and also no bone. Both Yates and Pivot brands turned out to be 100% pure blood and bone. This televised result led to significant changes in the law around Australia and the company manufacturing the fraudulent product went broke.

All of these rather boring bits and pieces prepared the way for organic growing of food in Australia. Finally, it was becoming much safer. Now we have the Biological Farmers Association accreditation of organic products (BFA). This is probably your best protection.

Standards Australia is producing standards for organic products. Sadly, even they are not going to investigate organic fertiliser labels. Perhaps the ACCC will do something one day.

TOP RIGHT: Forensic biologist, Derryck Klarkowski testing blood and bone on *Burke's Backyard* in 1994.

RIGHT: Many of the brands tested were impure or contained no blood or bone. Both Yates and Pivot brands turned out to be 100% pure blood and bone.

The bottom line

Food is much safer now. BFA certified products are pretty good. Be aware that you can't completely escape 'chemicals'. Horse poo probably contains some medicines occasionally: wormers, antibiotics, even pain killers. Much the same applies to all animal manures. All chemicals that get rid of intestinal worms in animals can destroy good worm populations in soils (although the chemicals do break down rapidly).

Your own garden soil can contain contaminants. DDT and its relatives have a half-life of around 15 years. So, if the concentration of, say, Dieldrin was originally 100 times the acceptable level.

- In 15 years it is 50 times too toxic
- In 30 years it is 25 times too toxic
- In 45 years it is 12.5 times too toxic
- In 60 years it is 6.25 times too toxic …. and so on

That is, some pesticides can hang around for a long time in the soil. If you are really worried, the Australian Government Analytical Laboratories (AGAL) can test your soil for these chemicals.

In areas near industrial sites (eg, cities) often you get small amounts of toxic pollution. When you use roof-water often this has traces of chemicals.

Having said all of the above, if you follow the general advice in this book, you will produce superb, safe food. If you grow from seed you could save quite a bit of money too.

This is a fun world of safe, tasty food that will give your children and grandchildren a very safe start in life. Meet and work with the neighbours and form a local community. Swap produce, exchange jams and preserves and spread recipes.

While growing vegies and fruit at home was a dangerous pastime 20 years ago, home garden systems, remedies and sprays are now very safe indeed.

What is organic?

In essence organic gardening or farming means the production of food (or other) plants and animals using natural systems and natural additives. It seeks to avoid synthetic chemicals altogether and concentrates on balanced, natural systems that promote healthy soil, plants and animals. So, natural fertilisers like animal manures, composts and rock, such as rock phosphate, are used. It is also acceptable to use unadulterated animal by-products such as blood and bone fertiliser.

Other ground-up rock minerals such as gypsum, lime and dolomite are acceptable. Natural insecticides (made from plant or animal extracts) such as *Baccilus thuringiensis*, which kills caterpillars, or pyrethrum, which kills sucking insects, or neem oil, which kills various insects, are acceptable.

In general, lateral solutions to pest control are preferred: eg, sticky, yellow boards to attract and kill insects, food lures in water in bottles to drown fruit flies, better timing of cropping and harvesting, biological control (predatory birds and insects), pest-resistant crops, companion plants, etc.

Be very clear on this: organic farming is a very, very good idea.

Biodynamics

Biodynamic farming was established by Rudolph Steiner through his lectures between 1922 and 1925.

Biodynamic farming has some organic value, but it is more a religion than a science. More like astrology than astronomy.

It recommends planting in rhythm with the planets. It also states that certain substances diluted 100 billion times will still benefit a crop. For instance, followers of this system bury a female cow horn stuffed with cow manure on the autumn solstice, then dig it up six months later on the spring solstice. Then the cow manure contents are taken out, diluted with a huge amount of water and applied to a large area of land.

As with homeopathy, I know of no scientific experiments that verify these practices. Curiously, Standards Australia is in the process of setting out standards for Biodynamic Farming. It's rather like developing sheet music for air guitars.

Abuse of organics

Not all natural things are super good. Arsenic, cyanide, digitalis and many other poisons are natural. Equally, lots of synthetic things are good for us—for example aspirin (a synthetic copy of a willow extract) and soap.

Some organic farming people are building a religion a bit like the biodynamic farming people. They have linked nasty chemicals to giant multinational companies who are claimed to be raping and pillaging the world. This sort of paranoia has no place in organic farming. These people have also linked genetically modified plants to the evil multinational plan. Mankind has genetically modified plants for around 10,000 years by hybridising species, creating tetraploids (eg, common wheat), and producing clones (all cuttings of plants—eg, grapes—are clones). The multinationals supply what people want and need. If anyone has created them it is all of us. Just as we have created pollution and greenhouse gases. As knowledge advances, so, hopefully we will all adjust our practices to ones that are sustainable.

Organic labelling

In Australia, the controlling body for organic certification here is AQIS (The Australian Quarantine Service). This is only because our exported foods must meet AQIS's National Standard for Organic and Biodynamic Produce in order to be sold to certain countries overseas.

AQIS has accredited a number of different (non-government) organisations and associations to certify organic foods. These groups are self-regulating. Until we get an Australian domestic organic standard from our government, these organisations provide the only system offering organic certification.

Organic farmers tend to have their produce certified by one of the bigger certifiers such as The Biological Farmers of Australia (ACO—Australian Certified Organic), and confirmed that they were subject to regular checks and measures. The main AQIS accredited organisations and their logos are listed below. Visit their websites for information regarding their individual organic standards. **NB:** if you a buying imported organic products they may display different logos pertaining to their country of origin.

Australian Certified Organic (Biological Farmers of Australia) www.aco.net.au

Bio-Dynamic Research Institute (BDRI) www.demeter.org.au

National Association for Sustainable Agriculture, Australia www.nasaa.com.au

Organic Food Chain www.organicfoodchain.com.au

Organic Growers of Australia www.organicgrowers.org.au

Tasmanian Organic-Dynamic Producers Cooperative organic.com.au/top/

Building and planting
an organic vegetable garden

Construction & soil preparation

Get this bit right, and vegetable gardening will be easy forever. Get it wrong and you may have constant troubles and pain. So take your time, plan it out and build a really good vegie garden

We met a family who were really keen to start an organic vegie patch. Teresa, a chef, had dreamed of having fresh produce from her own garden to cook for her partner Rob and their sons Luke and Matt; she also wanted her sons to experience the process of growing organic food. So we decided to help them build and maintain a great vegie patch and to share their journey. This book will help you do the same.

Location

All vegie gardens must be in full sun (all day). If you decide to create a really beautiful vegie garden (maybe a potager garden), then put it near the back door of

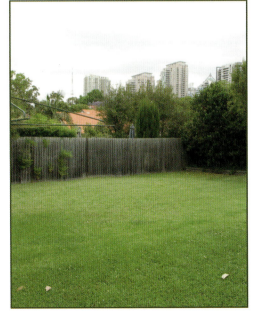

BELOW: A full-sun position is essential to grow vegies. We chose an area on the northern side of a fence that is bathed in sunlight all day.

the house for ease of harvesting and for its beauty to be seen. If you want a larger, less attractive vegie garden, put it up the back, away from the house.

The classic test of where to put the vegie garden is this: is the grass in that area lush and green? We chose an area for our garden on the northern side of the garden fence—note the lush green lawn indicating a full sun position.

Soil

You can't buy great soil in Australia. Don't be fooled by claims of 'organic premium garden soil' or whatever. In many areas of Australia (especially Sydney) the soils sold by nurseries and landscape supply companies are alluvial silts. These awful 'soils' are often mined from riverbeds. This damages the river systems and also produces soil materials that don't work well at all.

These silts often fail to develop proper soil structure (minute cracks mostly) that permits water penetration and gaseous exchange with the air. The soils are anaerobic, that is, your vegies' roots won't get enough oxygen to breathe and they won't grow well. Even the addition of organic matter such as compost doesn't help these alluvial silts much at all. I have been testing one area of premium organic soil mix for over 20 years. After all

BELOW: We contacted a pool company who were excavating a site a few streets away; they gave us the wonderful soil from their dig for free.

"When I first saw the soil, I thought it was crap! It didn't look like your traditional black, fine dirt. But looking at all the produce we've got, obviously it really works! That's what I've told my friends and they're doing that now too."
Teresa (mum)

this time, even with constant addition of organic matter, the soil still will not support healthy plant growth. About all that it will grow is plants suited to boggy, anaerobic areas such as paperbarks and bottlebrushes.

Your own soil is good. It is the best soil that you can ever get. Work that soil up with compost, manures, gypsum, etc and it will be perfect. So many people say that their soil is no good because it is clay. Clay soils are amongst the best soils in the world! Clay soils work up beautifully. Never ever let any of your soil leave your property. It is pure gold.

If others nearby are silly enough to get rid of soil, get it from them. This is what we have decided to do with our starting-from-scratch vegie garden because we needed extra soil for our raised garden beds. We contacted a swimming pool company and asked them if we could get some soil from an excavation near to our site. The company told us that they have to pay huge amounts to dump the soil. The soil was the sort of clayey rubbish that most gardeners would pay to get rid of too. If you look at the photo (right) you will see the orange colours of the clay in this soil. We got the soil for nothing and that saved the pool company the dumpage fee and lots of petrol.

As the soil was being unloaded I was so sad thinking of all the soil all over Australia that is discarded because people wouldn't buy beautiful recycled soil. People, sometimes, are quite mad. But I was happy that the soil was exactly what we wanted: rich, fertile and able to help to hold lots of water and with the capacity to develop perfect structure over time. It's a thousand times better than bought soils.

BELOW: Clay soils are good soils! Most people will tell you clay soils are rubbish. They're wrong.

Building and planting

> "Making mud and crushing rocks was the best."
> **Matt (aged 6)**

Preparing the ground

Next we planned out where our four raised vegetable beds would be positioned. Each bed is 3.6m long and 1.3m wide. The paths are 90cm wide to allow for wheelbarrows etc (see diagram).

When we were happy with the overall size and shape of the beds-to-be, we put stakes in the ground and set out the overall area with string lines. Then we marked the grass with marker paint, ready for the removal of the grass. We chose to remove the grass but you could spray it with Zero or Roundup, wait a week or two for it to die, then just turn it into the soil below.

To remove the grass, we rented a turf cutter from an equipment hire company. To achieve really straight edges, I cut out the overall shape with a sharp spade and removed the outer grass by hand. You need to sharpen your spade on a bench grinder first.

The turf cutter removed the grass beautifully. Some of the turf was retained for re-laying on the path areas later on, and the rest was used for general lawn repair and also donated to a neighbour to improve his lawn.

OPPOSITE: Every boy's dream, a pile of dirt of their own! Brothers Luke and Matt make the most of theirs.

FAR LEFT: We used stakes and string lines to set out the overall area.

NEAR LEFT: Marker paint shows where the grass was to be removed.

Building and planting

NEAR RIGHT: To achieve really straight edges, cut out the overall shape with a sharp spade and remove the outer grass by hand.

FAR RIGHT: A great tip is to sharpen your spade using a bench grinder.

NEAR RIGHT: Turf cutters can be rented from hire companies; they do a great job and can save you a lot of time.

FAR RIGHT: The turf is easily rolled up and can be used elsewhere in the garden or given to a neighbour. Tip: retain enough rolls to fill in the pathways between the vegie plots later.

Next we re-marked the corners of the beds-to-be and spread a 10cm layer of our new soil on top. Then we dug this over to the depth of a fork (around 8–10cm).

This was quite hard work the first time. Try to push the fork into the ground by standing on it, then use the handle to lever up the soil. Slowly work your way along, levering out the edge of the compacted soil as you go.

FAR LEFT: A layer of soil (from the swimming pool dig) is added, and forked in.

NEAR LEFT: The next layer is semi-decomposed horse manure and shavings.

FAR LEFT: The icing is a large handful of gypsum per square metre plus a sprinkling of Dynamic Lifter.

NEAR LEFT: Fork it all over so the soil is crumbly and all the ingredients are mixed in well.

On top of this we spread a 10cm layer of semi-decomposed horse manure and shavings plus a large handful of gypsum per square metre (and a sprinkling of Dynamic Lifter). This was forked over again. This time it was quite easy. Bulk horse manure and shavings are often available free from thoroughbred stables near racetracks.

ABOVE: ACQ treated pine is considered a safer choice for vegie garden edges as it does not contain arsenic.

ABOVE RIGHT: The treated pine edges are joined with galvanised screws.

Building the raised edges

We decided to construct the garden bed from the new ACQ (Alkaline Copper Quaternary) treated pine. This is considered a safer type of treated pine than the usual CCA product since ACQ does not contain arsenic whereas CCA does. There is no clear scientific evidence of problems with the CCA treated pine, it is just that we decided not to take the risk near food production.

The sleepers that we used were 2.4m long, 20cm wide and 7.5cm thick. We joined them by pre-drilling holes at the corners, then screwing them together with galvanised screws. To achieve the 3.6m length, we used 20cm long reinforcing rods as dowels after pre-drilling holes in the ends to join a half sleeper and a full one together. Then, for in-ground stability, we pre-drilled holes and hammered 50cm reinforcing rods through the timber and into the ground.

We installed three sides of each garden bed, then added another layer of new soil, horse manure, gypsum and Dynamic Lifter. This, too, was forked over, after which the fourth sleeper on each bed was screwed into position.

FAR LEFT: The lengths of treated pine were joined by pre-drilling holes and inserting 20cm reinforcing rods as dowels.

NEAR LEFT: The joined edges are then put in place, and secured to the ground using 50cm reinforcing rods.

FAR LEFT: The beds are then topped up with more soil, manure, gypsum and Dynamic Lifter and forked over again ready for planting.

NEAR LEFT: As a finishing touch, two archways and galvanised wire on the fence were added for growing tomatoes, beans, peas, etc.

Final touches

Finally, we erected two archways at the front and back of the north-south path. We also attached galvanised wire mesh along the fence to support climbing vegies such as beans, peas, etc. This is the beginning only of the soil management. Maintaining an excellent soil is a lifelong endeavour. Doing it organically, as

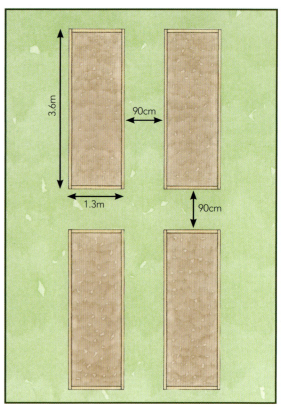

TOP LEFT: The completed beds. The grass will be relaid on the paths after the vegies are planted to avoid wear and tear.

TOP RIGHT: The layout for the four beds at Teresa's is simple. All four beds are the same size, 3.6m by 1.3m, with 90cm paths in between.

OPPOSITE: The dirt evolves with the kids, from a mud factory to a bike trail. The kids will remember this forever.

we have done, is more difficult but it is a wonderful investment in flavoursome foods and the family's future health. Please note that, at the time of writing, only the original formulation of Dynamic Lifter, available in 25kg bags or larger has the BFA organic certification. Gypsum is a naturally occurring mineral (calcium sulphate) and is organically acceptable. Animal manures may contain some chemical residues, but they are quite safe overall.

Important bit

Matt and Luke, the children of Teresa and Rob who own the garden, had a lot of fun with their dirt heap. As they grow older a dirt heap can change from a place for mud pies and matchbox toys to a ramp for their BMX bikes. It is every bit as healthy and as much fun for kids to have a dirt heap as it is to have a vegie garden. The ramp can be grassed over to look quite attractive in the lawn too!

"Rob thought it was a great idea, because he remembered playing in dirt piles as a kid too and said 'Boys love dirt, they need dirt. You're a girl, you just don't understand!'"

Teresa (mum)

Preparing for planting

While the best part of growing your own vegies is the picking and eating, the second best part is the planting—it's exciting and great fun, and kids love getting involved too.

Before you head for the garden centre to buy some seedlings and seed, the first thing to realise is this: you can't just plant whatever you like. What you can plant depends on the time of year. In the main, vegies can be divided into two groups: those you plant for warm-season harvest and those you plant for cool-season harvest.

Warm-season vegies are planted in late winter or early spring for picking in late spring and summer. You can often make a second sowing of these warm-season vegies in summer for harvest in late summer or early autumn.

Cool-season vegies are planted in autumn and early winter for harvest in late autumn, winter and early spring. You may also be able to make two sowings of cool-season vegies. See our handy wall chart at the back of this book for a simple guide on when to plant vegetables.

Building and planting

Two prime times to plant

There are two prime periods for starting crops in Australia (except in the tropics and subtropics): August to October for warm-season vegies, and March to May for cool-season crops.

Tropics and subtropics

Naturally, there's an exception to this planting time rule, and it applies in tropical and warmer subtropical areas. In the tropics and, to a lesser extent the warm subtropics, there's only one planting season and that is anytime out of the wet season. That makes the period mid-March to September your prime planting season there.

Shopping tips

Vegetables are sold as seedlings or as seeds in packets. Usually the vegie seedlings you see on sale at nurseries are the right ones to plant at that time of year. The only time you have to be cautious is during those change-of-season months—the last two months of winter and the last two months of summer.

Seeds are a different story. Displays may not be changed to reflect seasonal suitability but that doesn't mean you'll be caught out. Just look on the back of the packet where you'll find a sowing timetable or map for the seed-sowing times in your area.

Seeds or seedlings?

Both have their advantages and disadvantages and both have their uses.

Seeds: the biggest advantage of seeds is their cost. They are by far the cheapest way to raise plants and, as a vegie patch will contain quite a lot of plants, raising them from seed can greatly reduce your costs, making every plant you eat that much cheaper. Most vegie seeds are easy to sow right where they are to grow and, as long as you follow the sowing instructions, you'll usually get good germination and growth. Some seeds, however, are best sown into pots or trays of seed-raising mix and only transplanted into the vegie patch when big enough to handle.

This is more fiddly but not beyond your gardening abilities. If you want to avoid that sort of thing, read the instructions on the seed pack before buying. They will state whether direct sowing (into the vegie patch) is possible or if it's preferable to sow into pots first.

Seedlings: these are small plants which are sold in punnets of six to 12 or more plants. The cost per plant is quite a lot higher than for seeds, but then you're getting a germinated plant which is already about a month old. Vegie seedlings transplant quite easily into the vegie patch, although often you have to carefully separate individual plants which have been sown far too thickly by the growers—basil and parsley are examples of this and both are better planted as seeds.

Our tip—buy both

Many gardeners buy their vegies as both seeds and seedlings. Seedlings, being more advanced, will grow to maturity sooner than the same plants raised from seed. By planting a row of seedlings and a row of seeds, you'll get a longer period of harvest. In fact you'll get two lesser harvests rather than one big one, that might produce too many plants for you to eat.

Avoiding gluts

Working out how many of each vegie to plant is part of the art of growing your own, and avoiding gluts. It's wasteful to have too much of anything ready to eat all at once. When vegies are ready, they're ready and picking them later is no good—they'll be too big, too old, too tough and too bitter.

It's much better to work out how many of each item you actually eat each month (or each fortnight, for fast-maturing crops like lettuce) and then plant that number once a month or once a fortnight. That means you don't plant up your vegie patch all at once and you won't end up with a glut of produce.

Try to leave room for later plantings so you can be picking and eating one batch while another is nearing maturity and another still is half-grown. You won't have any wasteful gluts and, when the first batch is picked, you can clear that space and replant.

THIS PAGE: Prepare the soil very well, removing stones, weeds and other debris. Then work in lime, manure and compost and dig it all in well with a fork.

OPPOSITE PAGE. TOP LEFT: Rake the surface level.

TOP RIGHT: Make a shallow trench in the prepared soil with your finger.

BOTTOM LEFT: Drop the seeds in, spacing them as shown on the packet.

BOTTOM RIGHT: Poke large seeds in with your finger.

Sowing seeds

Seeds are super cheap. A whole packet only costs $3 or so and you'll get a lot of seeds in it. That means that each potential plant only costs a few cents and, in some cases, less than a cent each. There are two ways to turn seeds into plants; you can sow the seeds directly into the vegie patch or you can start them off in small containers and then transplant them into the vegie patch when they have grown a few centimetres tall.

Direct sowing

For direct seed sowing to be successful, first you need to prepare the soil. Dig over the soil until it's fine and crumbly. Remove stones, roots and debris from previous crops. Add lime, manure, compost and fertiliser if necessary and dig through thoroughly. Rake the surface smooth and level.

Make a shallow trench in the prepared soil with your finger, a stick or a trowel. Seeds need only be covered by their own thickness in soil so take care not to make the trench too deep.

Drop seeds into the trench at roughly the spacing indicated on the packet. You don't have to be exact about this and it's better to sow a few too many rather than too few seeds. When you have sown the length of row, cover the seeds over and gently firm down. Water in gently, so as not to dislodge the seeds.

Big seeds such as corn or beans can be simply pushed under the surface and covered over.

38
Building and planting

39
Building and planting

Sowing into containers

All sorts of containers are just fine for raising seeds. Pictured top left, small terracotta pots are fine, and a row of them filled with seedlings looks great.

Old egg cartons (top right) are good, too, and cheap as chips. Just sow one or two seeds into each egg cup.

You can recycle old butter, margarine or take-away food containers, but to provide the good soil drainage needed for seedlings, punch plenty of drain holes in the bottom of the container before adding the seed-raising mix.

Tiny seeds or the slow-to-germinate varieties are usually always best sown in pots for later transplantation into the vegie patch.

TOP LEFT: Almost fill the container with moist seed-raising mix or your own sieved compost.

TOP RIGHT: Level the surface then sow seeds thinly in rows. They have to be separated later, so don't overcrowd with seeds.

BOTTOM LEFT: Barely cover the seeds with more seed-raising mix or compost.

BOTTOM RIGHT: Label the seeds so you know which is which in a few weeks time. Use a pencil or permanent marker pen. Spray the soil well with a mister spray of water.

Tip: always keep the seed packet. It includes the spacing distances at which you'll need to plant out the seedlings when you transplant them out into the vegie patch.

TOP LEFT: Ordinary punnets are a simple, rectangular pot. Remove the seedlings by upending them onto your hand.

TOP RIGHT: Separate each seedling by gently pulling it away with its own share of soil and roots.

BOTTOM LEFT: Cell-type punnets are divided into individual plant cells. To remove seedlings, squeeze the base of the cell to push up the seedling. With cell packs, there is less root disturbance and they're easier to plant out.

BOTTOM RIGHT: Plant seedlings at the spacings stated on the label.

How to plant seedlings

Seedlings are planted into dug-over, fine, crumbly soil. Plant them in the late afternoon during the warmer months and always water them in gently, with a fine spray, once the batch is planted. Tip: if seedlings get too wet they might wilt—this is called 'damping off'. A spray of Yates Anti Rot might be worth a try.

Spring planting

With the raised beds and garden arches built, the wire netting attached to the fence and soil preparation complete, the garden is ready to plant out. Teresa and her family had never had a proper vegie patch before and so really enjoyed digging in and getting their hands dirty.

A planting plan of all four vegie garden beds is on page 52, but the simple summary is that we planted lots of family favourites that they already love to eat: tomatoes, salad greens, beans, corn, strawberries, eggplant, capsicum and zucchini, plus lots of herbs: basil, parsley, sage, mint, thyme and rosemary.

TIP: The best tomatoes. You can easily argue that cocktail tomatoes such as 'Tiny Tim', 'Sweetie', 'Small Fry' etc are the best of all tomatoes. They are fairly fruit-fly-resistant, fruit really heavily, are super hardy and self-seed naturally so that they come up free year after year.

TOP LEFT: Lay three stakes together so that the tops are level. About 30cm from the end, drill a hole through each stake. Push the stakes into the ground to form a triangle. Hammer the legs firmly into the ground.

TOP RIGHT: Push a length of wire through the drilled holes and twist firmly to hold the tripod together.

BOTTOM LEFT: Drill a hole through each leg at the same height and repeat at 20–30cm intervals until 50cm from the ground. Thread thick twine through the holes. Zigzag the twine down the tripod and tie off at the base.

BOTTOM RIGHT: Plant one tall-growing tomato in the middle of the tripod and one bush or non-staking tomato on either side of the tripod, but not between the tripod and the fence (which is the shady side).

Tomato tripods

Tall-growing tomatoes aren't strong enough to hold themselves up and need the support of 2.4m tomato stakes. We used six stakes to make two tripods, which can be a more attractive way to support tomatoes than a forest of single tomato stakes.

Planting out the beans

Where the vegie garden beds are against a wall or fence, start planting at the back and work your way forward. Don, Teresa and the boys started with climbing beans, planted and sown in a row along the base of one of the panels of wire mesh.

TOP LEFT: The soil here is a little on the acid side but can be made less so, and more to beans' liking, with a sprinkling of dolomite lime along the planting row—a handful for each metre is plenty. Dig it in.

TOP RIGHT: To plant seedlings, unpot each and place in a small hole dug in the row. How far apart you should plant them will be stated on the label. Tip: don't bury seedlings too deeply. Plant them at the same depth in the soil as they were in the pot in which you bought them.

BOTTOM LEFT: Seeds are much cheaper per plant than seedlings, and bean seeds are easy to handle and quick to germinate.

BOTTOM RIGHT: Just push the seeds into the moist, dug-over soil. Check the seed packet, but you only need to cover the seed with about twice the seed's thickness of soil or potting mix.

Building and planting

TOP LEFT: Labelling your seedlings is a good idea too.

TOP RIGHT: On the arch placed against the fence, we planted tomatoes. As the tomatoes grow taller, tie them loosely to their support or use plastic plant support clips (from garden centres).

BOTTOM LEFT: Plant sweet corn in blocks, not one long row. Block planting improves pollination so you get better cobs.

BOTTOM RIGHT: French marigolds aren't just pretty little flowers; their roots exude a substance which repels damaging soil nematodes. Dotting them around the edges of the beds makes a natural barrier with cheery blooms.

Wash your hands. Many seeds and bulbs are coated with fungicides during storage. So don't touch your face while handling them and always wash your hands afterwards if you aren't wearing gloves.

TOP LEFT: All vegies and herbs need room to grow and their share of sunlight. Be careful not to overplant the space you have. This is how the two back beds looked when fully planted on day one.

TOP RIGHT: If the day is sunny and quite warm, water in the seedlings as you go.

"We always do the watering usually, I like doing it 'cause it's sort of fun"
Matt (aged 6)

Planting a seedling

FAR LEFT: Unpot by tipping sharply onto your hand

CENTRE: Gently tease out any compacted roots

NEAR LEFT: Plant at the same depth as in pot, firm down and place label in the soil nearby.

Unlike other vegetables, tomatoes can be planted more deeply in the ground than they were in the pot. Remove the lower sets of leaves and plant the stem up to the first, remaining set. Roots will grow from the buried stem, making the plant stronger.

Building and planting

TOP LEFT: Grow the strawberries in pots—two pots for each boy, one inside the other. Start by almost filling the biggest pot with good quality potting mix, then partially burying the second, smaller pot inside the first.

TOP RIGHT: Add more potting mix to the lower pot and fill the upper pot as well. Repeat with the next set of pots.

Get the kids involved

Kids love the idea of picking the food they eat from their own backyards, so reward their interest with some special crops just for them. Strawberries are the ideal treats to start with, and because they don't take up much space, each child can have his or her own strawberries. Teresa's boys, Matt and Luke, love to compete with one another—so it was duelling strawberry pots!

BOTTOM LEFT: The boys were keen to plant up their own pots. Luke soon learned the knack of getting the plant out of its pot.

BOTTOM RIGHT: Doing is the best way to learn. Matt's doing a good job.

TOP LEFT: Matt makes sure that everyone knows which strawberry pot is his.

TOP RIGHT: Luke does the same as his brother, but in his favourite blue.

Easy name tags

You'll need acrylic paints and small brushes, plus a packet of screw eyes, some rope and two planks of timber. Teresa picked up some free offcuts from the local timber supply shop to use.

Let the kids paint their names on the wood then set it aside to dry.

To attach the name tags to the pots, screw in two small screw eyes to the back of the wood and feed through a short piece of rope to make a hanger.

The boys stuck a short stake into each of the pots, and hung the signs from the stake.

Teresa's vegie patch spring planting plan

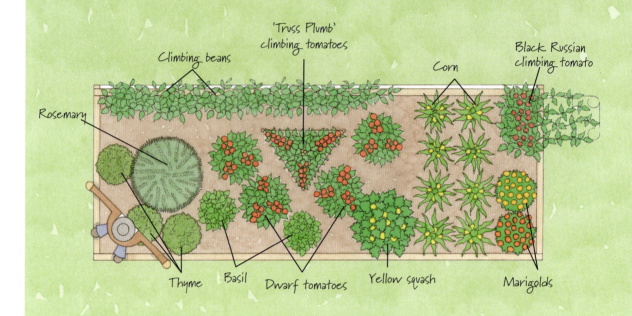

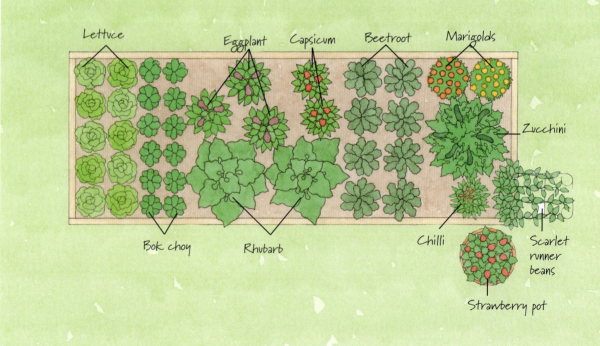

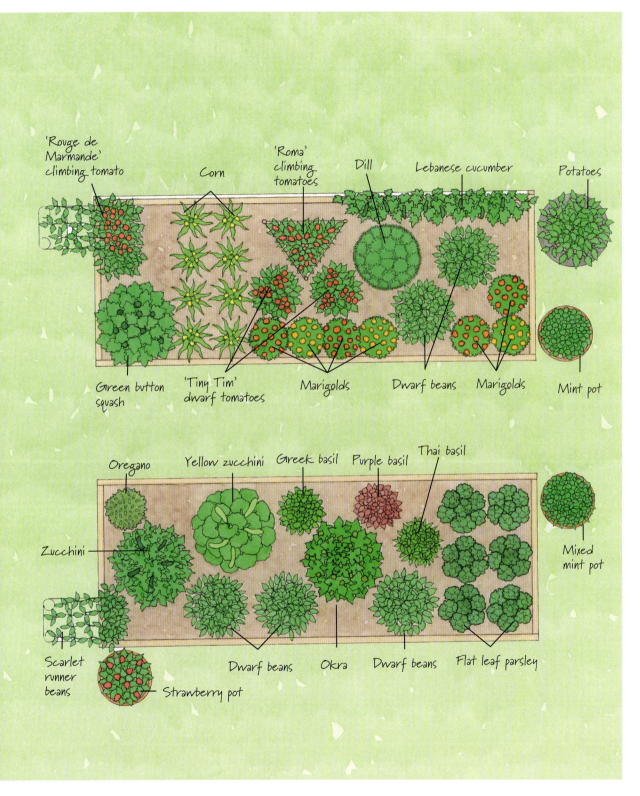

53
Building and planting

THIS PAGE, TOP LEFT: Just three weeks after planting and the beds are bursting with growth.

TOP RIGHT: Bok choy was stir-fry size and ready to pick.

BOTTOM LEFT: Zucchini were flowering and forming tiny fruits.

BOTTOM RIGHT: Beetroot, which we started from seed, had germinated and was growing strongly.

OPPOSITE PAGE, TOP LEFT: The eggplant had grown so tall it needed staking and tying

TOP RIGHT: The tomatoes had their first flowers

BOTTOM LEFT: Scarlet runner beans were off and running.

BOTTOM RIGHT: Vegies grow best when the soil is always lightly moist—never wet or dry.

Growth and routine care

Given good, fertile soil and regular water, vegies grow fast and that's the way you want it. This fast growth means quick harvests of sweet, tender and very delicious crops.

3 weeks after planting

54

Building and planting

Building and planting

4 weeks after planting

TOP LEFT, THIS PAGE: You'll be amazed at the rate of growth you get in spring. Plants seem to double in size each week.

BOTTOM LEFT: After seeds have germinated, you need to thin the seedlings out so that those remaining are spaced correctly (see the seed packet for spacing distances). Gently pull out unwanted seedlings. These beetroot thinnings were added to a salad for that night's dinner.

BOTTOM RIGHT: This zucchini is ready to pick. Don't let them get much bigger or they lose their flavour.

OPPOSITE PAGE, TOP LEFT: Corn powers away in the spring weather. It needs water and monthly feeding now.

TOP RIGHT: Keep the kids' potted strawberries moist and give liquid, organic fertiliser fortnightly.

BOTTOM LEFT: French marigolds bloom even more strongly as the weather warms up.

BOTTOM RIGHT: Weeds compete with vegies for water, food and light and they can also harbour pests and plant diseases. Don't let them get a foothold. Pull them out when they're this size and you'll never have a problem.

ABOVE: The first crop of lettuce and Chinese greens has been picked and the area (front right) replanted with more lettuce.

BOTTOM LEFT: Scarlet runner beans are clambering over the arch, flowering and starting to set pods.

BOTTOM RIGHT: Beetroot have grown to a size where they can be pulled up as 'baby' beets.

6 weeks after planting

TOP LEFT: In the kids' strawberry pots, snip off any runners as they form. This helps keep the plants flowering and fruiting.

TOP RIGHT: Bush beans, which need no support, are flowering and setting pods.

BOTTOM LEFT: Eggplant is starting to bear fruit.

BOTTOM RIGHT: Summer squash have grown so vigorously they spill onto the path.

"The red-flowering beans on the archway didn't produce that many beans but that didn't matter because they just looked so incredibly pretty."
Teresa (mum)

TOP LEFT: The corn is plump, sweet and ready to harvest. Tip: try a cob of corn straight from the plants. The raw kernels are so sweet and juicy you'll wonder why you bothered to cook them.

TOP RIGHT: The eggplant continues to flower so more fruit are on the way.

"Everyone just said wow this is the best corn ever! It was just sensational, it was really, really, really good corn."
Teresa (mum)

11 weeks after planting

BOTTOM LEFT: Bulging with produce—every vegie we planted is cropping now.

BOTTOM RIGHT: We have picked dozens of summer squash and zucchini.

TOP LEFT: Don says you need to know what you're taking on when you plant big, sprawling plants like pumpkins and zucchinis. Both plants are the gypsies of the vegie world—they like to wander!

TOP RIGHT: Luke and Matt are very impressed by these big zucchinis, but anyone who ate them wouldn't be. When they are this big they are tough and flavourless.

Beware

Pumpkins and zucchinis

Pumpkins, like gypsies, have a wanderlust. They wander hither and yon, so they need a large area to spread over. They are ideal if left to colonise a disused area of the backyard or a dirt heap. Ideally they need an area of at least 2m x 2m (ie, 4 square metres) per plant to produce sufficient fruit.

> "We loved the zucchinis to start with but by the end of it we were sick of them. The zucchini plant itself was amazing, I loved the flowers and watching it grow but it became enormous! It spilled over onto the lawn and was way too prolific at producing zucchinis! We had zucchini fritters, zucchini frittata, zucchini pancakes, zucchini cakes, zucchini chutney, in soups, you name it we had it!"
>
> **Teresa (mum)**

And see Teresa's amazing zucchini cake recipe on page 69.

Making a scarecrow

Making a scarecrow is a hoot and something the kids will love and always remember. There are no set rules but there are many, many ways to create and decorate your own guardian of the vegie patch. Teresa and her boys had a ball making theirs—here's how they did it.

Materials

- 1 x 160cm length of timber dowel for the arms
- 2 x 130cm lengths of timber dowel for the legs (the hardware store can cut all the dowels to length for you)
- galvanised wire (or any easily pliable wire you have)
- an old pillowcase or some plain fabric for the head
- fabric paint
- needle and thread (strong thread is best)
- 2m rope (any rope that's not too thick will do)
- straw and either newspaper, old plastic bags or Hobby Fill for stuffing
- some old clothes, hat, gloves and shoes
- 2m garden stake for support in the garden bed

The skeleton

Measure and mark the halfway (80cm) point on the longer piece of dowel.

Place the tips of the two shorter bits of dowel in an X shape over the halfway point and mark the junction point with a pencil. *Tip*: be sure to leave at least 15cm at the top of the X as this will form the neck and head.

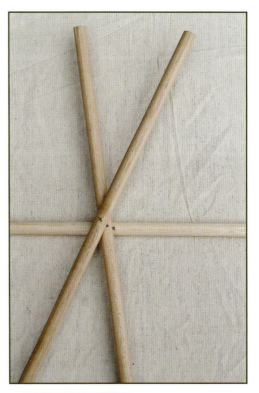

Drill a hole through each of the pieces of dowel where marked. Place the longer piece of dowel through the arms of the shirt and jacket, then wire together with the other two pieces of dowel using the holes you have drilled. *Tip*: if you don't put the shirt and jacket on first, it's very difficult to put them on once you've wired the timber skeleton together.

The head

Grab an old pillowcase or some plain fabric cut into a square approx 70cm x 70cm. Stuff with Hobby Fill, newspaper or old plastic bags and seal with a rubber band. Decorate the face as you like. We sewed on some hessian for the eyebrows and nose and painted the eyes and mouth with fabric paint (you can also use buttons).

Assemble

Find a good spot in your garden and hammer the garden stake into the ground. Put your scarecrow into position slipping the stake under his jacket.

Put the head on, by inserting the top bits of dowel into the rubber-banded head. *Tip*: tie the head to the dowel with some extra rope at the same point as the rubber bands, so he'll never lose his head on a windy day!

Building and planting

Put on his pants and button his shirt. Hand-sew his pants to his shirt so his pants stay up and the stuffing won't fall out.

Stuff the body with newspaper, old plastic bags, hobby fill or straw and put on his shoes. A bit more rope tied around the wrists and ankles is a good idea to stop the stuffing falling out (and it looks good too).

Pop some extra straw into the arms and pockets for a bit of charm. Put on his hat and gloves and give him a scary name.

Recipes from the garden

Chocolate zucchini cake

4 medium zucchinis
1 cup dried cranberries (Craisins)
2 ½ cups plain flour
1 ½ tsp baking powder
1 tsp baking soda
1 tsp cinnamon
¼ tsp nutmeg
180g 70% cocoa dark chocolate
2 cups caster sugar
4 eggs
¾ cup vegetable oil
1 tsp vanilla essence
1 cup buttermilk

Preheat oven to 180°C. Grease a deep round cake pan.

Grate the zucchini and gently squeeze out any excess liquid in a tea towel (it should measure 2 cups of zucchini), add cranberries. Sift the dry ingredients, except the caster sugar, into a bowl. Melt the chocolate on low heat in microwave. Beat the sugar, eggs and oil using a mixer on high speed. Reduce speed, gradually add chocolate and vanilla. Stir in flour mixture and buttermilk alternately. Stir in zucchini mixture. Pour into the cake pan and bake for 40–45 minutes. Test with skewer—it should come out clean. Sit in pan for 5 minutes before turning out onto a cake rack. Once cool, dust with icing sugar to serve.

Eggplant parmigiana

2 large eggplants
salt
½ cup olive oil
2 eggs
500g ricotta cheese
¼ cup grated parmesan cheese
½ cup chopped parsley
ground black pepper
1 ½ cups mozzarella, grated
1 quantity Tomato Sauce (recipe follows)

Cut eggplant into thick slices then layer in a colander and sprinkle with salt. Leave for one hour, drain and pat dry, then fry in olive oil until golden. Preheat oven to 200°C. Beat the eggs and add ricotta, parmesan, parsley and pepper. Into large baking dish, spoon in the tomato sauce mixture over bottom, cover with a layer of eggplant, then some ricotta mixture and mozzarella. Repeat the eggplant/ricotta/mozzarella layers, finishing with ricotta. Spoon over remaining tomato sauce and sprinkle with mozzarella. Bake for about 30 minutes. Serve immediately.

Tomato Sauce

1 kg tomatoes skinned, seeded and chopped
salt and pepper to taste
1 large onion chopped
2 cloves crushed garlic
large handful fresh basil, chopped

Place all ingredients into a large pot and bring to the boil. Cover and simmer for 20 minutes. Puree. You can either use the tomato sauce immediately or store in sterilised jars in the fridge for up to 6 months.

Zucchini relish

10 cups diced zucchini
4 cups chopped onions
5 tbsp salt
1 tbsp nutmeg
1 tbsp turmeric
2 tbsp celery seed
2 tbsp cornflour
½ tsp pepper
3 cups sugar
2 cups white vinegar

Place zucchini and onions in a large bowl, add salt and let stand overnight. Next day, rinse in cold water and drain. Place in a large pot and add all remaining ingredients. Gently simmer for about 30 minutes or until the mixture looks thick. Seal in sterilised jars, stores for up to 6 months.

Serving suggestion: This relish is great with any cold or grilled meats, hamburgers, cheese platters or on sandwiches.

Strawberry and mint sorbet

750g approx strawberries pureed to make to 2 cups, sieve out seeds
1 cup water
1 cup caster sugar
1 tbsp chocolate mint or apple mint or common mint, chopped finely
1 tsp vanilla paste or vanilla essence

Place sugar and water in pot on low heat to dissolve sugar, stirring constantly. Once dissolved stop stirring and bring to the boil for 1 minute. Remove from heat and cool to room temperature. Stir in strawberry puree, vanilla and mint. Pour into non-aluminium dish, cover with lid or foil. Freeze at least 8 hours or overnight, stir when getting slushy. Spoon into food processor and blend to a smooth texture. Quickly transfer back to container and refreeze for approx 4 hours. Serve in chilled wine glasses with extra berries and mint.

Vegie patch salad

2 large red banana peppers
2 ears of corn
2 tbsp rosemary-infused olive oil
1 large zucchini diced into 1cm pieces
1 clove garlic, minced
3 spring onions, chopped
1 tbsp chopped fresh thyme or lemon thyme
2 cups cherry tomatoes, halved
1 tbsp chopped fresh oregano
4 cups baby spinach leaves
salt and freshly ground black pepper

Roast peppers on a barbecue or under a grill until black all over, cool and remove skins and seeds. Dice flesh into 1cm pieces.

Cook corn in boiling salted water for 2 minutes, remove kernels from cob with a sharp knife. Heat olive oil in large frypan, add corn and zucchini and fry on med–high heat till lightly browned. Reduce heat and add peppers, garlic, spring onions and thyme, and stir for 1 minute. Transfer to a bowl and let cool to room temperature. Stir in tomatoes, oregano, baby spinach and season with salt and pepper.

Serving suggestion: this can be served on a bed of couscous or as is.

Rhubarb and hazelnut tart

Base and rhubarb
700g roughly chopped rhubarb stalks
²/₃ cup caster sugar
80g whole roasted hazelnuts
100g cold butter
2 egg yolks
1 tsp cold water
3 tsp sugar

Filling
4 eggs, lightly beaten
²/₃ cup caster sugar
2 cups thickened cream
1 tsp vanilla paste or vanilla essence

26cm flan or pie plate

Place chopped rhubarb in big bowl and sprinkle over ²/₃ cup caster sugar, stand for 3 hours, then drain in strainer. Preheat oven to 180°C.

   Place hazelnuts in food processor and blend; add butter, yolks, water and 3 tsp sugar. Process until the pastry balls around the blade. Wrap in cling wrap and refrigerate for 30 minutes. Pat pastry into flan tin evenly on bottom and up sides. Blind bake for 10 mins, remove paper and bake for a further 10 minutes. Spoon in rhubarb and bake for 10 minutes. Whisk filling ingredients together and pour over rhubarb. Bake for 40 minutes or until just set. Stand for 1 hour before serving. Sprinkle extra sugar and chopped hazelnuts on top; serve with Chantilly or whipped cream.

Sultana carrot cheesecake

Crust
1 cup digestive type biscuit crumbs
3 tbsp sugar
½ tsp cinnamon
3 tbsp melted butter

Filling
500g (2 pkts) cream cheese
¼ cup caster sugar
¼ cup brown sugar
½ cup plain flour
4 eggs
¼ cup orange juice
1 tsp orange zest
1 cup grated carrots
½ cup sultanas
½ tsp ground nutmeg
½ tsp ground cinnamon
¼ tsp ground ginger

Topping
250g (1 pkt) cream cheese
1 tbsp orange juice
1 tsp orange zest
1 cup icing sugar

Crust: Preheat oven to 150°C. Combine all ingredients in a bowl and when well combined, press into a 23cm spring-form pan. Bake for 10 minutes.

Filling: Combine 500g (2 pkts) of cream cheese, sugars and flour. Add the eggs one at a time, beating well after each addition. Stir in the orange juice, zest, carrots, sultanas and ground spices. Pour into baked crust, bake at 220°C for 10 minutes then reduce the heat to 120°C and bake for a further 55 minutes. Cover with foil if the top starts to brown.

Topping: Beat together 250g cream cheese (1 pkt), orange juice and zest. Add sugar and beat until smooth. Spread over cooled, cooked cake. Chill before serving.

Pumpkin and red lentil soup

1 kg chopped butternut pumpkin
1 cup red lentils
1 tsp grated fresh ginger or to taste
1 tbsp orange zest
1 litre vegetable stock
1 large onion, chopped
1 cup buttermilk
handful fresh sage leaves
butter, for frying sage leaves

Place the first six ingredients in a large saucepan or pot and season with salt and pepper. Cook uncovered on a medium heat until the pumpkin is soft. Puree. Check seasoning and add more salt and pepper if required. Stir in the buttermilk, serve into bowls and top with sage leaves fried in butter.
Serving suggestion: a teaspoon of buttermilk swirled into a pretty pattern looks great on top.

Bread rolls with pesto and oven-dried tomatoes

450g strong plain white flour
1 sachet fast action dried yeast
1 tsp sugar
1½ tsp salt
300ml lukewarm water

In a large electric mixer bowl, mix flour, yeast, sugar and salt. Mix in the water slowly using a dough hook for 1 minute then 4 minutes on medium speed or until smooth and elastic. Place in a lightly greased bowl and cover with a tea towel. Leave in a warm place for about 1 hour or until doubled in size. Transfer to lightly floured surface, divide into 12 balls and roll flat. Spread with pesto (see recipe below) and chopped oven-dried tomatoes (see recipe next page). Roll into sausage shape, make a knot and tuck ends under. Place in greased slice tin, cover and let rise until double in size, approximately 30 minutes. Brush with egg wash and place in oven at 220°C for 15–20 minutes or until golden brown. Remove and cool on wire rack.

Pesto

a couple of good handfuls of basil leaves (see note)
1–2 cloves crushed garlic
½ cup roasted pine nuts
½ cup grated parmesan cheese
extra-virgin olive oil (see note)
pinch citric acid
salt and pepper

In a food processor, combine basil, garlic, nuts and cheese. Slowly add olive oil and taste and adjust if need be. Stir in salt, pepper and citric acid. Place in a sterile glass jar, cover with oil and cap tightly. You can store it in the fridge for 1 week.

Note: you can vary quantities to taste, but start with 1 cup basil leaves and ¼ cup olive oil.

Oven-Dried Tomatoes

1 kg cherry tomatoes, halved
1 tbsp olive oil
1 tsp sugar
½ tsp salt
½ tsp paprika
2 tsp apple cider vinegar

Preheat oven to 60°C. Line a baking tray with greaseproof paper. Toss all ingredients together and place on the tray, with the cut side of the tomatoes facing up. Bake for approximately 6 hours or until the tomatoes have dried. Place in a sterile glass jar, cover with olive oil. You can also add rosemary and thyme stalks. Cap tightly if you wish to store. (Later the oil can be used for salad dressings etc).

Autumn planting

When autumn arrives, summer vegies start to decline. It's time to renovate the beds and replant with crops Teresa and the boys can harvest from late autumn through to early spring. A few of the herbs remain as permanent fixtures, such as the rosemary, thyme, parsley and mint pots, but for the rest, their time is up!

Your first job will be to clear out the remains of the summer crops. By the time autumn's cooler days arrive, the summer garden will be looking pretty tragic, so it's time to remove the exhausted plants and replace them with the cool-season crops. Though they are often referred to as being 'winter' vegies, you plant them in autumn.

However, before removing any plants, be sure to harvest any remaining produce!

TOP LEFT: The teepees were ideal supports for the tomatoes and can soon be re-used to support broad beans.

TOP RIGHT: All the remains of the plants are dropped into one of two compost bins. By next spring, they will have broken down into rich, dark, sweet smelling compost that can be dug through the soil before planting the next batch of summer vegetables.

LEFT: It's important to remove any young weeds and other seedlings so the beds are completely clear.

OPPOSITE PAGE, TOP LEFT: Use a garden fork to dig over the soil. This opens up and aerates the soil, allows you to break down any clods and to work in additional organic matter such as horse or chicken manure.

OPPOSITE PAGE, TOP RIGHT: Finish off the beds by raking smooth and level. The finer the soil the easier it is to sow seeds and plant seedlings. See our handy lift-out wall chart at the back of this book for best planting times for vegies in your area.

Clearing up and getting ready for planting

It's much better to completely clear out the whole summer vegie patch prior to doing your autumn planting. So, set aside an hour or three for some really good exercise. You'll find that if you prepared your original patch well in spring, all the old, tired vegies should come out of the ground quite easily. Weeding and digging are the two most important tasks now, so have a great workout!

Clods of soil. For thousands of years farmers have broken up clods of soil, hence the name clodhoppers. A well dug-over soil is always best for vegies. It takes about 5–10 years to develop a really good vegie garden soil. Continue to break up sods, add compost and manures and mix everything together. A truly friable soil is easy to plant seeds into and will produce rapid growth in plants and single, straight roots on carrots.

TOP LEFT: The wire mesh that supported beans and cucumbers in summer will carry peas through autumn and winter. Peas like a bit of lime, so a sprinkling along the base of the mesh will give them a great start.

TOP RIGHT: Peas come up fast from seed and all you have to do is push them into the dug-over soil at the intervals stated on the pack. It's best to sow peas into pre-moistened soil.

Peas

Peas love the cooler weather but because they're not heavy croppers, you'll need a few of them. We ran climbing peas along the back of both fenceline beds and also made plantings both sides of our two garden arches. We also planted self-supporting bush peas to ensure a heavy crop. As well as regular shelling peas, we planted sugar snap varieties which are eaten pod and all and crisp, sweet, snow peas.

On our two garden arches we planted seedlings of snow peas. Being already germinated and growing strongly, they'll be ready to pick a few weeks before our seed-raised peas.

For each vegetable, everything you need to know to plant it correctly is on the plant label. The same goes for seeds. It's all on the back of the packet.

TIP: Keep your clips. Plastic climber clips are available at nurseries. They make attaching climbing plants to supports both quick and easy. These clips can be collected and stored on wire mesh or other trellis material for later re-use.

88
Building and planting

TOP LEFT: Whole podded peas such as snow peas grow well in the cooler months, so we planted some at the base of the arches between the two garden beds.

TOP RIGHT: All the instructions you will need for how to plant the peas, including the distance they should be spaced apart, are on the label that comes with the seedlings.

Feet first. All great vegetable gardens start with your feet. If you can't get your feet near the plants, harvesting is miserable and dangerous (think of all the stakes if you fall!). So keep your vegie gardens narrow— no more than 1.2m wide and put in some stepping-stones or pavers. This allows you to step into the garden to pick climbers such as beans, peas and passionfruit.

"Putting those paving stones in made so much difference! When we had all those tomatoes you just couldn't get in there. So having the stones in the middle to give you a bit of standing space is brilliant!"
Teresa (mum)

Building and planting

TOP LEFT: Leeks are a good value crop that have a long season of harvest. To plant leek seedlings, push a finger deeply into the prepared soil and drop the seedling in. You can bury up to half the length of the little seedling.

TOP RIGHT: To plant onion seedlings, first make a shallow trench.

Onions, leeks, shallots

You can grow early, mid-season and late maturing onions for an almost continuous crop of these kitchen staples, and you can raise them from seed or bought seedlings or a mixture of both for an extra-long season. Include leeks and shallots and you've the foundation for many of the family's favourite meals.

BOTTOM LEFT: Break the punnet of seedlings into smaller clumps before carefully separating the individual seedlings for planting.

BOTTOM RIGHT: Place them in the trench at the spacing indicated on the label. For shallots, make a 3cm-deep trench and simply lay the seedlings in it. Cover the roots, water in and in a day or two they'll be standing up.

Building and planting

TOP LEFT: Easy to grow from either seedlings or seeds, beetroot is an eat-it-all crop: you can eat the leaves and the roots.

TOP RIGHT: Carrots are a crop we like to start from seed. Sprinkle thinly into shallow trenches and lightly cover. They'll be up inside 10 days and you can start harvesting baby carrots 10 weeks later. With all seeds, mark where you've sown them with a label so you know what they are.

Root vegies. Turnips and swedes, parsnips, carrots and beetroot can all be grown through the cooler months. The great advantage of root crops is that you can pull them as you need them—the rest can stay in the ground to grow a little bigger.

BOTTOM LEFT: Broad beans aren't climbers but they do grow tall and need some support. Hammering in a stake at each corner of the broad bean planting will let us run supporting twine around the whole bed when needed. The plants within will also help support each other.

BOTTOM RIGHT: Broad beans are big, easy to sow seeds. They're very reliable, so don't waste money on seedlings.

Building and planting

Teresa's vegie patch: autumn planting plan

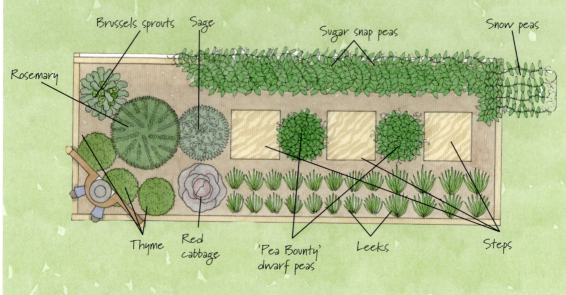
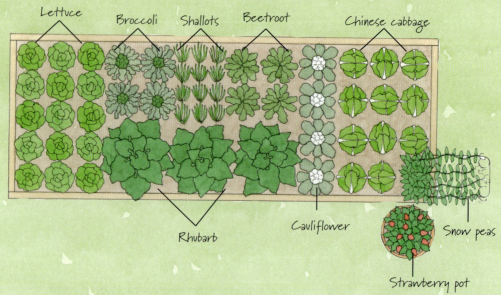

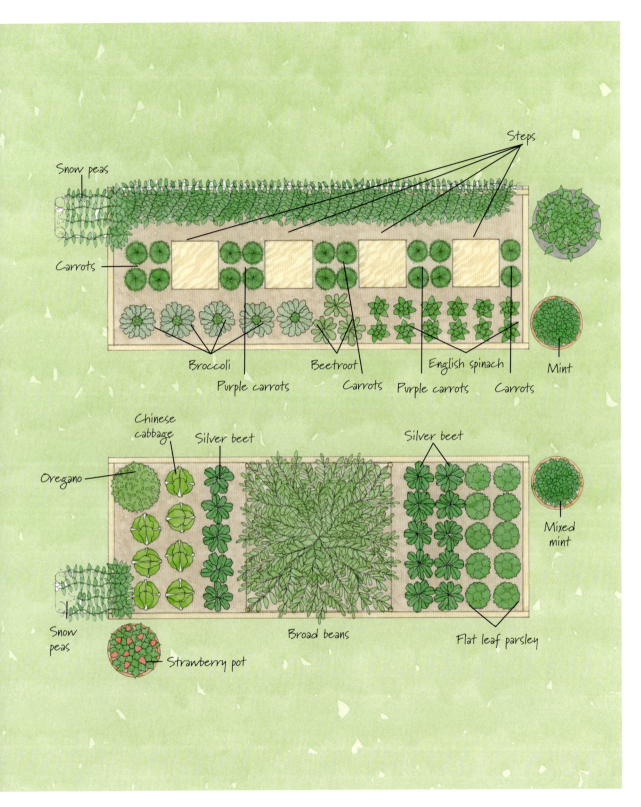

TOP LEFT: Broccoli takes about three months to reach picking size and should be kept growing quickly with light applications of fertiliser once a month. A plant food formulated for flowers is best.

TOP RIGHT: Cauliflower grows in much the same way as broccoli. To keep the curds white, fold two or three leaves over the developing heads. You can snap them at their centre vein to achieve this.

The cabbage family

The cabbage family can also be referred to as brassicas and as well as cabbages it includes broccoli, cauliflower, Brussels sprouts, kale, Chinese cabbages and Chinese greens such as bok choy. Most are easy to grow and do best in the cooler months.

BOTTOM LEFT: Chinese cabbage grows much more quickly than regular cabbage yet can be used in exactly the same way. With Chinese cabbage, you can have several crops in the same time it takes an ordinary cabbage to mature.

BOTTOM RIGHT: Liquid food (a mixture of water with Seasol and Nitrosol) will give the new plants an extra boost along.

7 weeks after planting

Blessed with plenty of warm, sunny days and good rain, the autumn crops romped away, some to the point of picking.

Along with regular silver beet, we planted a batch of the coloured stemmed varieties, sometimes called Swiss chard (pictured centre right). After seven weeks, the outer leaves are ready for picking and the plant will continue to grow. You can pick regular, white-stemmed silver beet the same way.

Leeks (pictured bottom right) are also slow to mature but you don't have to wait until they're as thick as those you see in the shops. Pencil leeks can be pulled after about 10 weeks. These aren't quite ready yet.

TOP LEFT: Look at the growth on the snow peas! They've almost reached the top of the wire trellis. There have been plenty of flowers on the snow peas resulting in pods that are pretty close to pickable.

TOP RIGHT: The growth on the broccoli is amazing, too! Some heads are almost ready for picking, meaning we'll be able to plant at least two more batches.

BOTTOM LEFT: The cabbages fell victim to the caterpillars of the cabbage white butterfly and though still edible, the warm autumn weather has made the heads looser than is ideal. For quality produce, spray plants with organic Dipel or Success once a week from the moment you plant them. Spray both sides of all leaves.

> "Rob and the boys head straight to the snow peas when they get home from school. They eat so many straight from the vine there's barely any left to cook for dinner!"
> **Teresa (mum)**

Support for broad beans

Anticipating the need of support for the broad beans, we placed four stakes around the planting site when we first sowed seven weeks ago. Now all we do is run twine around all four stakes to make an outer square and then run two diagonal lines forming an X in the middle.

Possum problems.
The parsley has remained as a permanent fixture in the vegie patch since summer but the possums love it and are determined to eat it all. Teresa and Luke came up with an ingenious solution. The guinea pig run they use to allow the guinea pigs to nibble on grass during the day, made the perfect possum-proof cage to cover the parsley at night. Problem solved.

14 weeks after planting

ABOVE LEFT AND RIGHT: Pulled, washed and straight to the kitchen. Plucking your home grown carrots from the ground is quite exciting.

LEFT: The early white onions, though still small, are big enough to sample. The rest will remain in the ground to fatten up for a few more weeks.

OPPOSITE LEFT: You can pull leeks at any size from thumb thickness to fully grown. We grew leeks from both seeds and seedlings, so we now have them at various sizes.

OPPOSITE RIGHT: Harvest broad beans when they're young and small then eat the whole pod or wait until the pods fill out and extract the sweet, nutty beans from inside. Broad beans are a good value, high yielding vegie.

How to grow potatoes.

Potatoes are grown from 'seed' potatoes, which you can make yourself or buy at nurseries in late winter and spring. Lay out the seed potatoes in the shade until short green shoots appear and cut into sections with at least one sprout on each piece. Plant in 30cm-deep trenches dug into good quality, fertile soil. Place each seed potato about 40cm from the next. Cover with about 5cm of the soil excavated from the trenches. When shoots appear through the soil let them grow to about 30cm then half bury with more soil. Continue to do this as the plants grow, keeping them lightly moist. You don't have to add fertiliser if the soil has been prepared with manure and fertiliser. The potatoes are fully mature when the leafy tops of the plant have died off.

Staying organic

Harvest and storage

Yippee—harvest time!
The best thing about growing your own vegies is picking and eating them—harvest time! That fresh, home-grown flavour is hard to beat. Here are some tips on how to tell when your crops are ready to harvest, and how to store them so they last as long as possible.

Here's the good news: with a lot of home-grown vegies, all you need to do is pick them from your garden when they look just like the ones sold in the shops. The only difference is that yours will taste better.

This is true for vegies such as beans, zucchinis, snow peas, broad beans, spinach, silver beet, lettuce, onions, shallots and spring onions, but with others you'll need to learn a few simple little tests to do before you start harvesting. All these tests are easy enough to do and will help you get more value from your crops and all your hard work growing them.

Also, there are a few ways you can test whether fruit is ripe and ready to eat, so we'll show you those tips, too.

Once you've harvested your vegies there are many good ways to store them so they last the longest possible time, and there are some wonderful traditional methods of preserving your crops so they last for several months or longer, and we'll explain how they work, too.

Harvest early: young and tender vegies

All of the vegies listed here taste their best when you harvest them early, when they are still small, young and tender. In fact, the flavour of some of these vegies gets worse the bigger they grow, so don't put off harvesting them.

Asian leafy greens

When to pick: buck choy, choy sum and gai laan are fast-gowers and it's best to harvest them when they are 15–20cm tall, which is a bit smaller than the size sold in the shops. Their flavour is terrific then. If you have several plants and only need one, just harvest the largest one and leave the rest in the ground until needed a few days later.

How to harvest: pull up the whole plant and knock off soil from the base, before taking inside for preparation.

Storing tips: these leafy greens should be eaten as fresh as possible, but they will keep for a few days in the crisper section of your fridge.

Button squash, cucumber, zucchini

When to pick: all three of these are much better eaten small, rather than large. Harvest zucchini at 10–15cm size, which is smaller than the size they're usually sold at in shops, as they taste better the smaller they are.

How to harvest: cut off fruit at the base with a small sharp knife. Do wear long sleeves, as zucchini plants in particular are very prickly to be around.

Storing tips: all of these can be kept in the crisper section of the fridge, uncut, for up to five days.

Lettuce, mixed salad greens

When to pick: harvest these over a number of weeks, but older plants will tend to produce bitter leaves.
How to harvest: to pick just a few leaves from a plant, always pick off the larger, outer leaves, and leave the smaller, inner leaves to keep on growing. You can at any time harvest a whole lettuce plant if you like.
Storing tips: salad greens will keep in a plastic bag or container in the crisper section of the fridge for two or three days if leaves are dried well.

Rocket, mizuna, mustard

When to pick: All have a mildly peppery taste when young, but if you let plants get too big that mild peppery-ness will become a hot and unpleasant taste. So, harvest them young, when just 8–12cm high.
How to harvest: either pick leaves by hand from the outside of the plant, or use a pair of scissors to snip off the number of leaves needed.
Storing tips: these salad greens should be kept and stored the same way as you store lettuce.
Big tip: don't grow too much! While their peppery flavour is a great component to add zing to a salad, it can take over, so you don't need a lot. Instead, sow small crops of these fast-growers fairly often, about four to six weeks apart.

Radishes

When to pick: while radishes are a great plant to get kids interested in gardening, because they grow and crop so fast, it's a shame the flavour is so peppery! The rule with radishes is simple: 'smaller is better'.
How to harvest: pull out whole plants when small and slice them into salads.
Storing tips: radishes keep well for several days in a plastic bag or container in the crisper section of the fridge.

Staying organic

Easy-going crops—harvest early or late

All of these vegies are wonderfully versatile. You can harvest them early on when they are at 'baby' size, but you'll get best value for money and still get full flavour when left to grow to the normal size they are sold at in shops. Or you can harvest most of them any time in between—when you like!

Beetroots, carrots, parsnips

When to pick: all three of these vegies can be harvested quite early when baby-sized, medium-sized or later on, when at the full size you see them sold in the shops. For example, if you have sown too many seeds and plants are growing too close together, just wait until they get to a size where they are almost getting in each other's way, and 'thin out' the crop, pulling up every second plant to make room for the others to grow on. Beetroot reach maturity about three months after sowing seed, and so you can harvest plants anytime between about six weeks after sowing seed, and three months. Depending on the variety chosen, carrots take between three to five months to reach maturity after sowing seed. Parsnips are slowest growers and will take months to reach full size.

How to harvest: beetroot are easiest to harvest than carrots and parsnips, as they partly poke out of the ground when mature, and so pulling them out of the ground is easy. Carrots and parsnips sometimes won't pull up easily if the soil is a bit heavy or compacted by rain, but they will pull up easily from the lighter, free-draining soils they prefer. If carrots don't pull out easily, use a hand-fork to loosen the soil around them, then pull. Experienced growers know that parsnips taste sweeter after they experience some cold weather, so try to time your parsnip-growing so you harvest the fully mature crop after your coldest months.

Storing tips: all three vegies can be left in the ground for a number of weeks, so only harvest as many as you need for dinner that night. In the kitchen, store them in a dry, cool, dark spot for several weeks or, if you prefer, in the crisper section of the fridge.

Broad beans

When to pick: there are two good times to eat broad beans—when they are very small and look like any other ordinary green bean, or when they are fully-sized, like the ones about 18–25cm long which you see in the shops (this is about 18 weeks after sowing seed). You eat the small baby broad beans whole, like any other bean. But you'll need to shell the large, mature pods and eat only the large inner beans if you're harvesting mature crops. Broad bean lovers say you should shell the large beans, too, to get just the tender, delicious inner bean. (To do this, drop the shelled beans into a pot of boiling water and leave them there 1 minute, then scoop into a bowl of cold water; the beans' outer skins then slip off easily.)

How to harvest: to harvest broad beans, snap off each pod at the base with your fingers. You should be able to harvest broad beans from one plant over a period of about four weeks. Start harvesting early, picking the larger pods, but leaving the smaller ones on the plant to keep growing to full size, for harvesting later on.

Storing tips: baby broad beans should be eaten soon after harvest, as they are at their tenderest and best then (a lot of people don't even bother to cook them, they are so sweet and tender to eat raw). Fully mature broad beans keep well in their pods for several days, but it's advisable to put them in the fridge if you are thinking of not cooking them immediately, as this will increase their storage life.

Capsicums

When to pick: these can be picked when fairly small, young and green, or leave them to ripen fully to red and harvest then. The flavour is sweetest when ripe and red, but green capsicums still have a juicy,

107
Staying organic

pleasant flavour sliced raw in salads or as an ingredient in cooked dishes. It's best to harvest only as many capsicums as you need for each recipe, and leave the rest on the plant.

How to harvest: snip each fruit off the bush, using scissors or secateurs, to avoid damaging the plants.

Storing tips: capsicum skin should be well dried (use a paper towel) before storing in the vegie crisper of the fridge in plastic bag or container. However, they will only keep there three or four days, so aim to use them soon after harvesting.

Chinese cabbage

When to pick: also called wombok or wong buck, the Chinese cabbage is a great Asian vegie. This is a type of cabbage, but it's smaller and a bit faster-growing than the big European cabbage. You can harvest Chinese cabbage from when they're about 18–20cm tall (that's half the size you see in the shops), through to when full-sized (about 30cm tall).

How to harvest: pull up the whole plant each time.

Storing tips: Chinese cabbage keeps well unrefrigerated as a whole cabbage for several days at room temperature or in the fridge, but once cut, keep in the crisper section of fridge.

Onions

When to pick: most growers leave their onions to reach full size, but you can pull them up earlier than that if you like. It's easy to tell when they're reaching maturity, as the leaves will start to die off (this is about four months after the first green shoots appeared above the soil). However, after onion plants have been growing above-ground for about two months, you can harvest some plants, when they are known as spring onions. Their flavour isn't as strong, but sometimes is very nicely sweet—perfect in salads.

How to harvest: pull up whole plants as needed. After harvesting

Bananas—the ripe stuff. Putting a ripe banana in a bag with an unripe fruit really does help to speed up the ripening of your fruit. Ethylene gas within the ripe banana is given off, trapped inside the bag, and gets into the unripe fruit, speeding up its ripening process.

mature onions, hang them up in a dry but airy place (eg, under a verandah) to let the bulbs dry fully for a week or two, prior to storage.

Storing tips: red onions keep for only a couple of weeks, but white onions have much better keeping qualities and brown onions keep the best. The ideal way to store onions is in an open-weave bag that allows plenty of air circulation, but failing that, keep them in an open-weave basket in a dark, dry part of the kitchen or pantry.

Peas, snow peas, sugar snaps

When to pick: whole pod peas such as sugar snaps and snow peas can be picked as soon as they reach the size sold in the shops. Generally, they're at their best when small and tender, so start picking as soon as they start cropping, as this encourages more pods to form and you'll get a better crop. With podded peas, remember that they're usually ready to harvest around three to four months (12–16 weeks) after sowing seed, so around the three-month mark, pick a pod, open it up and see what's happening. If the peas are small, let them grow on another week or so, and check again. Some podded pea varieties crop a bit earlier than this (10 weeks) so always keep your seed packet as a handy reference guide to harvesting times.

How to harvest: peas come off the plant quite easily if you gently tug them off by hand at the base.

Storage tips: sugar snap peas and snow peas will keep for a couple of days in the crisper section of the fridge, but if you're growing your own, it's best to pick and cook them on the same day. Podded peas are a similar story—best fresh—but they keep a bit longer in the fridge than the wholepod peas, and shelled, podded peas freeze well after being quickly blanched in boiling water.

Potatoes

When to pick: spuds give you a long period of time when you can harvest them. You can harvest baby potatoes when the tubers are small (cocktail potatoes) or you can wait until they are fully mature ('old' potatoes), or in between (ie, 'new' potatoes).

Simple test: potato plants start to form tubers (potatoes) after they finish flowering. A few weeks later, the plants start to die back. At this stage, you'll find small to medium sized 'new' potatoes inside the hill of soil where the plants grow. A few weeks beyond then, the whole plant dies back. At this stage you'll get the best crop of potatoes. But you can leave potatoes in the soil even after that, and they're still OK to harvest (although wet conditions can spoil crops left in the ground).

How to harvest: keep an eye on plants and note when they finish flowering. A week or two after that, go 'bandicooting'—this is fun! Tunnel into the hill of soil around the spuds with your hand, and feel around with your hand until you find enough spuds for dinner. To harvest mature 'old' spuds, you can pull the whole plant out of the ground, but always check carefully through the soil to find any spuds you might have missed.

Storing tips: potatoes keep well left in the ground. After harvesting, bring them inside and keep them away from all sunshine, but don't wash them—leave some dirt on them—it helps protect them from sunlight, which turns them green. Store them in a cool, dark place. If the temperature is too warm, they may sprout, so check them regularly. If they turn green they are poisonous, so either plant them back in the garden (the poison will disappear) or throw them out. Any potatoes that shoot can also be planted out.

Pumpkins

When to pick: most people wait until their pumpkins are at full size before harvesting them, but you can pick them any time you like, even when fairly small and they are known as 'baby squash'.

Simple test: to tell when your pumpkin is fully mature, keep an eye on the vine, where it attaches to the pumpkin. When the vine starts to wither, becoming wrinkly and woody, that's the time to harvest them.

How to harvest: use secateurs to separate each pumpkin from the vine, and leave a few inches of stem attached to each pumpkin.

Storing tips: prior to storing pumpkins, 'cure' them by drying the skin in the sun for two weeks. Put them in a sunny spot during fine weather, and let the skin harden in the sun. Bring them inside if rain is likely. Always store whole cured pumpkins on their sides, so moisture from dew cannot gather in the centre, around the stem. Some varieties of pumpkin, such as the hard-skinned Queensland Blue and Jarrahdale, will keep for months, once cured. Other varieties, such as the soft-skinned Butternut and Jap, don't keep for very long, and so you should aim to eat them soon, within a couple of weeks at best. If any pumpkin is showing signs of rot, cook it straight away. Turn excess pumpkin into pumpkin soup to freeze, and your storage problems—and casual winter meals—are taken care of. Once cut, store pumpkins in the crisper section of the fridge, where they'll keep for five more days.

Shallots/spring onions

When to pick: These can be harvested one at a time, if you like, and leave the rest in the ground until needed. They keep well over several weeks once near mature size. You can harvest these when they are smaller than the ones sold in the shops—say, at pencil-thickness size. However, as they get older their flavour does get a bit stronger.

How to harvest: these usually come straight out of the ground easily if you hold them at the base while pulling, but in doing so you can sometimes disturb the plant next to them, so take care.

Storing tips: it's best to store these vegies out in the soil in the garden, but if you have some to keep inside they store fairly well at room temperature for a few days, or in the crisper section of the fridge. However, in the fridge they can become slimy if kept in plastic bags for more than three days.

Harvest when ripe

Lots of fruits and some vegies should be harvested when they are fully ripe. Here's how to tell when your crop is at the peak of perfection.

Apples

When to pick: you'll have to make sure which apple variety you're growing, as there's a long season over which apples ripen, depending on the variety. Apples vary so much that some ripen just three months after flowering (these are the 'early season' apples), while others (the 'late season' apples) can take six months. But here's a good thing to know: the 'late-season' apples have the longest storage life, and the 'early-season' apples have the shortest storage life—you should eat these soon after picking.

Simple test: one good, simple way to test if your apple is ripe is to pick one by giving it a light twist. If it comes off the tree easily, it's likely to be ripe, or close to it. The next test is the taste test. If it tastes a bit sour, it's not ripe, so don't pick any more. Leave the rest on the tree. In fact this 'taste test' is your best guide. If one apple on your tree isn't ripe, the others won't be, either. Fruit size isn't a good guide, but once you are used to your apple crop after a few years, the ripe fruit colour might become familiar to you and be a handy extra guide to ripeness.

How to harvest: ripe apples should come off the tree with a light twist of the hand, so that's all that's needed. However, if harvesting from your backyard tree, it's best to do this as a two-person team, with one person holding the step-ladder or ladder while the other harvests. Safety should be your main concern!

Storing tips: late-season apples are the best ones to store. Pick them just before they reach full ripeness, discard (or eat straight away) any with blemishes or skin damage, wrap each in tissue paper and store separated from each other in a cool, dark spot.

Early-season apples: Gravenstein, Vista Bella.

Mid-season apples: Gala, Bonza, Jonathan, Red Delicious, Golden Delicious.

Late-season apples: Granny Smith, Pink Lady, Red Fuji, Lady Williams, Jonagold, Sundowner.

Citrus
Mandarins and oranges

Simple tests: both mandarins and oranges can be orange-coloured and look ripe, but still taste sour. Equally, they can be greenish yet quite sweet. Your best guide with these two sweet citrus varieties is to do a taste test. Try just one fruit, and if it's sour, leave the rest on the tree and they will sweeten up over the next couple of weeks.

Sweet tricks: you can help fruit sweeten up with a few tricks, though. One is to cut back on watering the tree, and do another taste test next week, and the week after that. The lack of water will concentrate sugars in the fruit (but don't let the plants go so dry that they wilt). Another tip from old growers, to bear in mind next season if this season's crop wasn't up to scratch, is to sprinkle a tiny amount of copper sulfate (about 1 level dessertspoon to a mature tree, spread over the entire area under the canopy) and water in well, and this will help to sweeten up your crop of oranges or mandarins. Be warned that mandarins taste very bland if left on the tree too long.

How to harvest: use a pair of secateurs to remove the fruit from the tree to avoid splitting or tearing branches or bark.

Limes and lemons

When to pick: too easy, just pick them when they're fully grown and the right colour—ie, when limes are green and lemons are yellow.

How to harvest: use a pair of secateurs to remove the fruit from the tree to avoid splitting or tearing branches or bark.

Storing tips: it's best to leave citrus on the tree and just pick them as you need them. However, remember that limes don't store as well on the tree, losing their limey flavour over time, so try to use them up fairly soon. Lemons are much better left on the tree. Mandarins can become puffy and dry if left on the tree too long, so harvest and eat them fairly soon. Oranges keep on the tree well, but if you leave them there so long that the weather warms up, they can turn green again! They'll be sweet inside, just green on the outside. If picking citrus to bring indoors, make sure their skin is dry (eg, leave them in the sun for an hour) before storing them in a basket in the kitchen. Eat them or use them within the next four or five days, though. You can also store citrus for a few weeks in the crisper section of your fridge, but they produce their best juice and taste better at room temperature. And you can also preserve citrus juice, especially lime juice, by freezing it in ice-blocks, then storing the blocks in a plastic bag or container in your freezer.

Corn

When to pick: home-grown corn has a wonderful flavour, but this is one crop that you ought to eat at its best, as it doesn't keep for very long.
Simple test: fortunately, there is a simple test for corn-ripeness. First hint of ripeness is that the silks at the top of the cob will look dry and brown. Next test, pull away a few leaves from a cob and push your thumbnail into a kernel. If milky fluid seeps out, that's the perfect sign the corn is ripe. Start harvesting!

How to harvest: cut each cob of corn off at the base with a sharp knife.
Storing tips: corn cobs keep at their flavoursome best for just a few days, but they will survive in the fridge for a week or two, slowly losing quality each day.

Garlic

When to pick: when the tops of the plants start to wilt and die off, it's ready to harvest.
How to harvest: pull up the whole plant then hang it up somewhere airy and dry (eg, under a verandah or carport) and let the bulbs dry fully for a week or more, until the base is crinkly and papery, before using.
Storing tips: once fully dried, garlic can be stored for a number of weeks if kept in a dark, dry, airy place. A string bag is handy for keeping onions and garlic, so too an open-weave basket.

Ice-cube method: All sorts of herbs and fruit juices can be stored in ice-cube trays, but you can soon run out of trays if you try this with them all. So here's the trick. Put the minced-up herbs or lime juice or lemon juice or whatever you plan to freeze into the trays, let them freeze overnight, then tip out all the cubes into a plastic bag or container, so your ice-cube trays are free again for their next assignment.

Green beans

When to pick: you can pick green beans before they reach full size, but you'll get better value for money and the same great flavour, if you let them reach full size. Older beans, however, can become stringy, and aren't that good to eat. If the beans are the right size, 15–20cm long, they're ready to eat.

How to harvest: pick by hand, holding the bean at the base and snapping it off the plant with a bit of stalk attached.

Storing tips: beans will keep well in a plastic bag or container in the vegie crisper section of your fridge for several days. They can also be frozen well, if blanched in boiling water prior to freezing. Another way to store them is to cook a casserole, soup or other dish containing beans, and freeze and store that.

Rhubarb

When to pick: late summer and autumn are harvest time in cool and temperate zones. Stems can be harvested year-round in warmer climate zones. However, it's best not to harvest stems from plants when they're young (ie, less than two years old). After that, rhubarb plants will crop well for several years.

> **Home-dried herbs.** Home-dried herbs are underrated in cooking (they can be great at times) but they also make nice gifts, including potpourri. To dry any herbs, tie them in large bunches and hang them in a dry, airy spot that won't be affected by rain but will catch some breezes. Depending on the weather, it could take a week or two for them to dry. Check the inside of the bunch, as well as the outside, before you decide they're ready. Good choices for drying include oregano, marjoram, thyme, rosemary, sage, mint, bay leaves and lavender.

Just pick stems when at the size sold in shops (ie, 30–40cm long). Colour isn't a great guide, as green-stemmed rhubarb tastes just as good as traditional red-stemmed rhubarb.

How to harvest: only harvest a stem or two from each plant at any time (so grow two, three or many more plants for a steady supply of stems). Don't take too many from the one plant as this will weaken the plant—and rhubarb plants will keep on cropping for you for many years, if well cared for. Harvest by pulling stems downwards and outwards sharply from the base, or cut off stems at the base with a knife.

Storage tips: rhubarb stems will keep in the vegie crisper section of the fridge for just a few days, but it's best to cook rhubarb soon after harvest, and only harvest as much as you need each time.

Tomatoes

When to pick: colour is your best guide to the ripeness of a tomato. Wait until tomatoes start to show some colour in the fruit before thinking about picking them. Some people like to ripen their tomatoes indoors at this 'early-colour' stage, keeping their tomatoes in a dark, dry spot indoors to let them fully ripen. They do this primarily to keep the ripening tomatoes away from attack by fruit fly and birds. Others say the fruit tastes better if allowed to ripen on the plant, but this ripening fruit does mean you'll have to keep a close eye on the fruit to prevent those pest attacks. It's your call as to whether you harvest early or harvest late. Just go by colour and only eat when fully ripe, but we do guarantee you that your home-grown tomato, no matter how you decide to ripen it, will taste better than the ones you buy in your local supermarket. **Big mistake:** don't ripen your tomatoes on sunny windowsill. Always ripen them in a dark spot indoors, away from direct sun.

How to harvest: ripe fruit should come away with a gentle tug when fully ripe, but if you're harvesting them part-ripe, cut them off with scissors or secateurs, to avoid damaging plants.

Storage tips: once ripe, tomatoes keep well for several days indoors, but if the fruit is becoming over-ripe either keep them in the fridge for a few more days, but use them soon, or turn them into a sauce you can freeze. Tomatoes themselves don't freeze well.

Watermelons

When to pick: the colour of the underside of the watermelon is a good indicator that it's ready to eat. It will change to yellow when it's ripe.

Simple test: tap on the fruit with a knuckle of your hand, it should give a hollow sound.

How to harvest: cut the melon from the vine with a knife.

Storing tips: uncut watermelons will keep well for a week or two, but once cut store them in the fridge, where they will last for another week or so. This is not a long-lasting fruit, so enjoy it when it's at its best soon after harvest.

Hey pesto! If you have a glut of basil, turn it into pesto then freeze the pesto. See our pesto recipe on page 83

Preserving

Beyond the hard-working crisper bin and the freezer inside your fridge, there's a big, wonderful world where home-grown fruits and vegies can stay fresh and tasty forever—in preserving jars. Lots of organic gardeners are rediscovering the joys and big savings of preserving your own produce, so check out our rundown on how to get started.

Bottling

Fruits and vegies with a high water content, such as tomatoes, beans, peaches, nectarines, plums, apricots, apples, pears and many others are ideal for preserving in bottles or cans.

Getting organised: it's vitally important to get well organised with bottling, as getting it wrong can be a health hazard, or at the very least lead to a major mess! So, you'll need to keep the bottles and lids sterile and preferably buy new lids for the jars (re-using lids can be risky if they don't provide a perfect seal), and always take care during the stage when you're applying heat to the jar full of preserves. That said, there's plenty of good advice around on how to do it, and Aussies for generations have been doing it beautifully, so there's no reason you can't either.

Fowler Vacola: there's one name in preserving produce that everyone knows, and that's Fowler Vacola. This company can supply everything you need, and they can be contacted on (03) 9329 7799, if you want to find the nearest stockist of their

products. They can supply the complete home preserving kit for you, and also make sure to get their excellent book, *Secrets of Successful Preserving—Fowlers Vacola Instruction & Recipe Book*. Another good source of preserving kits is ebay (www.ebay.com.au) but with the recent popularity of home preserving (and organic vegie gardening) you might find the competition on ebay can get hot at times!

The basics: fruit and vegies for bottling should be firm, young and never overripe. While you wash and prepare the fruit, discard any blemished or bruised fruit or at least cut away any blemishes if they are only small. You can leave small fruits whole, but cut larger fruits, including those with pips or stones, into halves or quarters. Fruits with a thicker skin, such as apricots and peaches, should be peeled, and apples and pears should be peeled, cored and sliced.

Sterilising pan: after the bottle is packed with preserves and syrups or other liquids to enhance their flavour, and the special lids attached, the next step is to apply heat to the jar in a sterilising pan. Inside the pan, the jars need to be completely submerged in water and elevated off the bottom of the pan on a wire rack. One of the main things to watch for is not letting bottles come into direct contact with the hot base of the pan or the bottles will crack. Lots of old hands wrap an old tea towel between the bottles to stop them knocking against each other and the pan.

Pickles, relishes, chutneys

When you eat an olive you're enjoying a pickled fruit, and all sorts of fruit can be preserved in pickles, and there's more than one way to pickle a fruit. An olive, for example, is pickled in brine, which is very salty water. Dill pickles and gherkins are cucumbers preserved in a brine solution.

Relishes are prepared using chopped fruits and/or vegetables cooked in a spicy vinegar solution. Depending on the taste they want to achieve, cooks can add anything from sugar (for a sweet relish) through to chillies (for a spicy relish), plus various aromatic and flavoursome spices. (See Teresa's zucchini relish recipe on page 72).

Chutneys are from the subcontinent most famously, and they are relishes in which fruits ranging from mangoes to tomatoes and others are turned into a relish flavoured with herbs and spices.

Equipment needed: all you need is a recipe book, as creating pickles, chutneys and relishes is nothing more than another form of cooking that follows a recipe—and you do it on your cooktop mostly. However, as with any preserved foods which you intend to store for a long time, it's absolutely essential to store the final product in a perfectly sterile glass jar with a sterile lid. While many pickles, chutneys and relishes keep well at room-temperature, unopened, it's best to keep them in the fridge after the jar has been opened.

Jams, jellies, marmalades

As making chutneys, pickles and relishes is a form of preserving food by cooking them in the kitchen, so is the art of making jams, jellies and marmalades. The magic ingredient in jams, jellies and marmalades is sugar. So these are all sugar preserves.

What's the difference between jams, jellies and marmalades? Easy. Marmalade includes the fruit and the finely sliced skin. Jams include the fruit, but not the skin. And jellies contain no fruit or skin, and are the strained juice made from cooking the fruit and skin.

One big thing you need to know about when making sugar preserves is the substance called 'pectin'. This helps the liquids to thicken and set. Some fruits are naturally rich in pectin (for example, cumquats and quinces), while others aren't (for example, strawberries). However, a lack of pectin isn't a problem for home cooks, as the product 'Jamsetta' (available in supermarkets) can help fruits low in pectin (such as strawberries) make lovely jams.

The remainder of making sugar preserves is simply following the recipe, and using sterile glass jars when storing the products.

Drying

While people have been drying foods to preserve them for thousands of years, these days the process is so much easier if you buy a home food dryer. But if you love the idea of preserving foods on the cheap, all you need is sunshine (and a couple of fine days).

Sun-drying: make up some drying frames by covering an open timber frame with flyscreen wire. Spread thinly sliced fruit or vegies on the netting, leave it in the sun

for a few days and you'll have beautifully sun-dried tomatoes, apricots or other delicious fruits. Sounds easy? Well, the drier and hotter your climate, the easier it is, but it can get tricky on the humid East Coast. But in Perth, Adelaide, Alice Springs and areas inland, it's well worth a go. Remember though that the drying food needs to be protected from dust and flies, and covered at night to avoid dew. Here's a good tip: stand the legs of drying frames in shallow dishes of water to stop ants getting at the food.

Machine dryers: food drying using a machine designed for the purpose, such as a Sunbeam Food Dehydrator, priced around $100, is quicker and a lot easier than sun-drying (but more expensive).

Oven drying: if sun-drying didn't work for you and you're determined not to buy a machine dryer, try your oven. Set your oven to its lowest temperature, maybe even prop the door open to lower the temperature, and test-dry a couple of batches and see how you go.

Drying basics: use only ripe, unblemished, perfect fruit and vegies (or at least remove any bruises or blemishes). Wash and drain, then thinly slice them. Place in rows, close together, one layer deep, on the drying rack. When dried, pack in air-tight containers or vacuum-sealed bags.

Vacuum packing

Vacuum packing is a relatively modern form of food preservation, which works by extracting all air from specially designed bags and canisters to create a commercial quality seal, which prevents oxygen and moisture from affecting the flavour, texture or nutritional value of food. What you need is the correct gear, such as a Sunbeam Foodsaver VAC660 (around $249).

Sterile jars. Clean, sterile glass jars are a must for preserves. Wash jars and lids clean and rinse in hot water. Submerse them in boiling water for 10 minutes, then dry on paper towels.

The art of compost

Let's talk nothing but complete rot for a while! Compost is a wonderful thing, but some people have trouble making it, and this chapter is for them. Read our tips, give it another try, and second time round it will work!

Let's start at the other end of composting. What's so good about compost, and why should you bother making it? Well, compost is the single most important aspect of long term success with vegies. It is also by far the best soil improver/conditioner. All soils are eco-systems composed of fungi, bacteria, insects, worms and many other life forms. Compost is the fuel that drives populations of these organisms. As compost breaks down it becomes the driver of soil structure—millions of invisible cracks in the ground. This provides air to plant roots, without which most plants die.

Compost is the basis of all organic gardening and it releases nature's own fertiliser. It gently feeds all plants that grow in it. That's not bad for starters. And it's free fertiliser, too. Once you get the hang of making it, you'll save a packet on bought fertiliser. That's pretty good!

Dry repairs

For starters, compost helps to maintain a soil's moisture level, and that's what everyone needed to help them through the savage droughts of recent years.

When soils become extremely dry they just won't absorb moisture no matter how much you water them. These soils are called 'hydrophobic'—it's as if they're scared of water. Compost can help these very dry soils to absorb moisture once more. It's magic stuff.

How does it do it? Compost is almost a living thing. It's full of little, living, beneficial micro-organisms that you might not be able to see, but they're there. These micro-organisms help to remove the waxy coating that forms around each grain of extremely dry soil. It's this waxy coating which prevents a hydrophobic soil from being able to absorb water any more, but when you dig plenty of compost into this very dry soil, it starts to absorb water again. Sure, modern wetting agents are also terrific in helping a soil absorb moisture again, but compost is the age-old soil doctor, too.

Clay and sand

Gardeners with heavy, rock-like clay soils might think they have a very different problem when compared with gardeners with light, nutrient-deficient sandy soils, but they actually have a lot in common. They both need to add lots and lots and lots of compost to their soils. The good old soil doctor, compost, will bring both soils closer to the middle, to the more ideal loamy type of soil that holds moisture, is easy to dig, is a great place for worms to live and raise worm families, and has plenty of nutrients for plants.

Gardeners with soils that are already in that good, loamy middle ground should just keep on adding compost every year, so their soil stays healthy and gets better every year.

We are told by scientists that one inch (2.5cm) of soil takes 500 years to form. In nature this is often true, but this is a very misleading statement. In gardens or on farms you can dramatically improve soils or create new soils in one to three years. You can rapidly create excellent soils to a depth of 30cm by adding organic matter and water to crushed rock, coarse sand or rubbishy soils or clay sub-soils.

For the less physically able (or the busy or bone lazy) using spoiled lucerne hay or pea straw instead of compost is really easy. Bales naturally pull apart into 'biscuits' which are around 8cm thick. Lay these on top of your ground and watch the worms create perfect soil. Spoiled hay is the blackish stuff exposed to the weather on the outside of stacks, or just hay that rotted and is useless for livestock. It is usually around one quarter the cost of high quality hay.

TOP RIGHT: A biscuit of lucerne hay.

TOP LEFT: Lucerne is an excellent mulch for vegies.

Compost and vegies

Digging compost into your soil prior to planting out a new bed should become a routine for all organic gardeners. Compost might be a good, gentle food but it does need a helping hand to keep greedy, fast-growing vegies happy, so that's why you should also add in extra fertiliser, such as manure, when preparing vegie beds.

RIGHT: A bit of manure as well as your compost, keeps fast-growing vegies happy.

Staying organic

Other uses

But while we're singing the praises of compost, we might as well check off its other virtues before we get onto the art of making your own.

Mulch: you can use compost as a mulch. Just lay it over the soil and it will feed plants.

Potting mix: you can use compost as potting mix too, but you'll need to combine it with other ingredients. Here's the recipe for home-made potting mix:

4 parts compost
1 part shredded sphagnum moss
2 parts coarse river sand

Liquid fertiliser: you can turn compost into batches of liquid fertiliser, too. Add one part compost to three parts water in a bucket or tub, give it a good stir and leave it for three days. Strain the liquid and use it as fertiliser on any plants in your garden. *Tip*: adding a capful of Seasol to the liquid turns it into a good soil conditioner. You can make three or four more batches of fertiliser from the same initial batch of compost, and when it has run out of puff just add the residue back to the compost heap—the ultimate in recycling.

Cheap as chips

So, if you were wondering why you need compost, all those reasons start to add up, don't they? Now, you can throw your money away and go and buy some bags of ready-made compost from your garden centre, or you could get some delivered in bulk, but the cheapest and best compost is the home-made stuff. Once you get the hang of making it, you'll be making big batches, free of charge, every year.

Bin basics

Two bins are ideal: one of the most common composting options now is some kind of plastic compost bin. These are perfectly OK for making compost, but our first tip is this: get two of them. When one bin is full of scraps, clippings and cuttings, it will take a few months to become compost, and that's why you need a second bin—it's where you put the scraps and clippings when the other bin is full. The same applies if you are building your own bins from timber, wire, galvo or whatever else you have at hand. Build two, at least.

Bin size: a pretty good rule is 'the bigger the bin, the better', but if you're cramped for space don't let that bother you too much. Just buy the biggest bin which is practical for your garden. Tumbler style bins don't take up much space. They have a number of virtues which we'll tell you about in a moment, and they come in a range of sizes, so check them out.

The ultimate: in large gardens where space isn't a problem, you could build the ultimate composting set-up and have a couple of large compost bins, each at least one cubic metre (ie, 1m x 1m x 1m) sitting there side by side. This magic number of one cubic metre is important because compost bins actually heat up inside. You might already know about our native mound-building birds such as scrub turkeys and mallee fowl. These birds build huge mounds of leaves, just like enormous compost heaps, and lay their eggs in the mounds. The heat from the decaying leaves incubates the birds' eggs. Backyard compost heaps do the same—they heat up inside. However, the bigger the heap, the greater the amount of heat within a heap. And at around one cubic metre it gets seriously hot in the middle of the heap. Poke a stick into one and you can see steam coming out. This amount of heat makes the composting process quite rapid but there's an important bonus—it will also kill off weed and vegie seeds. So the compost which comes out is the best because it's seed-free.

Best position: most people put compost bins where you can't see them, for good reasons. They're never going to win a beauty prize. But the warmer the spot you find for them, the better. It would be great if you could put your bins out in a sunny spot, as that will help the bin heat up and that extra warmth will speed up the composting process. But in many gardens all the sunny

spots are already taken up with vegies, herbs and flowers, so compost bins come last when it comes to occupying sunny spots. The other important thing with siting your compost bin is to at least put it where it's easy to get at. You should be adding stuff to your bin every few days at least, so if it's a long distance from the kitchen, or hard or messy to get at, you'll soon give up on adding to it. So try to find the warmest, least ugly spot close-ish to your kitchen, and put your bin there. Is there somewhere down the side of the house, for example?

Most people never bother but it is critically important to regularly turn your heap (once a month at least). This means digging it over thoroughly with a fork. An unturned heap can take over a year to rot down, but a turned heap is ready in two to three months.

Build your own: if you want to build your own compost bins on the cheap, go ahead. (And see our DIY tumbler bin, on page 139). There are plenty of designs available online, so have a go at making your own. Just think about how you're going to protect your heap from rats and rain, and make it easy to turn over the heap with a fork.

Tumbler bins: one of the main jobs in speeding up composting is adding air to the heap, and that's the big advantage of tumbler-style bins—they make it easy to turn over the heap. Compost tumblers are by far the best of all compost bins for small gardens. With daily rotating (ie, spinning the barrel) the compost is ready to use in three to four weeks. In the typical garden compost heap, material can take six to 18 months to fully compost. The reason is that most people can't or don't want to turn their heaps regularly. It's the turning that speeds breakdown of the organic matter. Untended heaps just sit there and do little apart from stink.

Digging over (turning) your compost regularly aids faster breakdown.

Essentially, compost tumblers are drums suspended on a frame that allows you to rotate them at your whim. You don't get dirty or smelly and the job takes a few seconds. This is by far the fastest composting method. It also has the advantage that the best designs allow a wheelbarrow to slide in under the drum so that the contents can be simply poured into the barrow.

Another great advantage is that these bins are rat and mouse proof. Many conventional compost heaps form high rise apartment blocks for rats and mice who eat your scraps and raise their babies in the warmth of the heap.

The disadvantages of compost tumblers are:
- They are expensive, averaging around four times the price of say, a standard plastic compost bin.
- You probably still need a standard plastic compost bin as well to store the next batch of scraps etc while the current batch is composting away. When you empty the tumbler, in goes the next batch from the standard bin.
- They are a bit sweaty. You need to balance the mix of your different ingredients carefully. Too much wet stuff like kitchen scraps and grass clippings and it all goes smelly and gooey because of too much moisture.
- They don't make the heap very hot inside, and so vegie seeds (such as from pumpkins, tomatoes, cucumbers) will survive composting and come up when you spread the compost around the garden. The solution to this problem is to avoid adding seeds to the bin in the first place, but that is easier said than done, sometimes.

There are several compost tumblers on the market ranging in price from $200–$700. Some of the cheaper ones are too low to fit a wheelbarrow underneath, to unload your compost into. So keep an eye out for higher, horizontal tumblers, which are easier to unload. eBay is also a good hunting ground for compost tumblers and you might just bag a bargain!

There are other options:

Sit-on-the-ground plastic bins: the cheapest bins are the el-basic black plastic bins with a lid, which sit on the ground. Sometimes these are given away free by local councils, so the price is right! These are OK, but they're hard work most of the time. Their big disadvantage is that it's hard to turn over the

heap. You could reach down into the heap with a garden fork and give things a poke, or lift the bin off the whole heap, then fork it all back into the bin. But what most people do is nothing, and that sort-of works, as everything will eventually compost down, except it will take months, maybe years, to happen. For that reason, these basic bins can suffer more easily from the two classic compost bin problems of being either wet and smelly, or dry and dusty or, worst of all, neglected entirely.

Aerated bins: Getting air into the heap is crucial. Turning the heap over is one way to do it, but you might consider an aerated bin. If you get some agricultural pipe and poke it into the heap, it will aerate it. Agricultural pipes have a lot of holes in them and these holes will aid aeration of the heap. You can run a couple of pipes vertically down from the top of the heap or horizontally in from the sides. You can also purchase ready-made aerated bins such as the Aerobin.

What goes in

Anything that was once a living thing can be composted down, if you give it enough time, but you can't put Uncle Arthur there, that's against the law (even if it was in his will). Same for Socks the cat and Rex, too. It's against the law and it smells crook, too.

So, as long as you don't add any meats of any sort, any vegetable matter at all can go into your compost bin.

Good choices
- fruit and vegie scraps and peelings from the kitchen (minus the seeds if you can manage it)
- lawn clippings

- garden trimmings and prunings
- shredded newspaper
- old garden mulch or straw
- fallen leaves
- old potting mix
- ash from the fireplace
- coffee grounds, tea leaves
- cow, horse or chook poo, or leftovers from old packets of manure
- blood and bone
- the odd handful of dolomite lime
- the odd spadeful of garden soil (magic ingredient!)

Bad choices
- cat or dog poo, or kitty litter (can harbour harmful viruses/diseases)
- cooked food with possible meat content
- diseased or dead plants (can spread the disease later on)
- diseased or spoiled fruit (can spread grubs, insects, etc)
- anything that wasn't a living thing (plastic, metal, glass etc)
- meat or bones

Smaller is better

As composting is all about breaking down former living things into even smaller particles—so small they end up looking like soil—it makes sense to give things a head start by making everything you add to the compost heap as small as possible in the first place.

In practice, this means you should at least aim to cut up prunings as much as possible, and maybe chop up bigger vegie scraps (such as tough old pumpkin peelings or whole vegies) so they break down faster.

Just add air

Remember that the main thing most compost heaps need is air. The more you remember to tumble the tumbler, or fork over the contents of your bin, the better. The microbes which break everything down inside a compost bin are little living creatures,

and they need air to breathe, just like every other living thing. So do what you can to give them plenty of air. Air is also the most important thing in soils and potting mixes. Without air, plant roots don't survive. Compost and organic matter help provide air in both the soils and potting mixes. Water is the other thing which the composting process needs to work and sometimes that's the source of the biggest mistake made in composting—either too much or too little moisture. Read on…

The biggest mistake!

Here's where lots of beginner composters go wrong—they don't add enough variety to their compost bin. Adding too much of the one ingredient can cause all sorts of problems within a compost bin. To work well, you'll need to add a fairly balanced mixture of so-called 'wet' ingredients, which are rich in nitrogen, and 'dry' ingredients, which are rich in carbon. It's a bit like baking a cake, you need wet eggs and dry flour to get a lovely cake, and you'll need a good mix of wet nitrogen and dry carbon to bake up a good batch of compost, too.

Wet ingredients
- freshly dug weeds
- manures
- fruit and vegie scraps
- lawn clippings

Dry ingredients
- straw (or some stable manure composed mostly of wood shavings or straw)
- paper
- autumn leaves

Too wet? If your compost heap seems a bit moist and smelly, it's time to increase the amount of dry stuff you're adding to the heap. Shredded newspaper is a quick fix, autumn leaves are fantastic, and if you raid your bag of straw mulch and toss in a few handfuls of that, it will help balance things up. Also, add in a spadeful or two of our magic compost fixer—garden soil. It's full of microbes and maybe some worms, and a spadeful or two can

really get things happening again if the heap has slowed down. **Too dry?** On the other hand, if the heap is too dry, you could just sprinkle on some water and mix that in, but also add in a few handfuls of Dynamic Lifter if you have some to spare, plus some extra kitchen scraps or garden clippings and work them into the bin or heap. And yes, add a spadeful or two of garden soil to dry heaps, too. It will help to get things going again, too.

Smelly dramas

Compost bins usually start to smell if you've been neglecting them, or the balance of wet and dry ingredients is a bit out of whack. If you have mistakenly added meat scraps to a bin, that's your smelly problem right there. The smell should subside fairly quickly, but be sure not to do that again. If meat scraps aren't a possible problem, then here's what to do:

Turn over the heap: give the tumbler a spin or get out the garden fork and turn everything over. Often the smelly-making bits are at the very top of the heap, and the problem disappears when they disappear from sight, deep down into the heap.

Adjust the moisture level: if the bin is wet and smelly, add more dry ingredients, and work them into the bin. Check that the cover on the bin fits, and that rain isn't making it all too wet. If the bin is dry and smelly, turn over the heap first, and add some moisture or some wet ingredients.

Give it time

Once your compost heap or bin is really full—chockers—it's time to switch over to filling up the spare bin, and give your full bin/heap some time to break down and become a batch of compost. In summer this might happen rapidly, in just a month or two, and in winter it might take a bit longer. While you wait for it all to break down, lend a hand by keeping on adding air (tumbling the tumbler or forking the heap). Don't add anything new to the full bin (even if it drops a bit in level as it breaks down), and in a few months you'll have a complete bin-full of beautiful compost, ready to go.

The ideal

So, what should your ideal batch of compost be like? Lovely, of course! It should be a rich, dark colour, crumbly in texture and with a pleasant, earthy smell. Just like really nice, top quality soil. You shouldn't be able to see anything which looks recognisable, such as leaves, vegies or whatever.

Worm farms

The popular alternative to a compost heap is the worm farm, and they're a great space-saver, plus the kids will be endlessly fascinated to have their own box full of scrap-munching pet worms to check on. They're a bit gross, but great at the same time!

It's easy enough to get started with a worm farm, too. Kits that provide everything you need, including the worms, are sold at major garden centres and hardware stores. It really helps to read

the instructions a couple of times to set it up properly, and follow their recommendations about feeding and care as closely as possible.

A lot of people experience similar frustrating problems getting their worm farms up and running as others do with getting compost heaps going. Some beginner worm farmers say they can't get them to work properly and they smell bad, others say the worms all died, or they simply discover that looking after a worm farm is more work than just tossing in your fruit and vegie scraps every now and then.

Special needs

Mild temperatures: positioning your worm farm so it doesn't heat up in the sun is vital, as overheating can kill the worms. A shady spot is best for them.

Favourite foods: worm farm worms won't eat everything. They have their likes and dislikes, and can even be fussy eaters, so it's very important to feed them what they like. Most fruit and vegie scraps are fine (but not their 'hated foods' see below) or as are used teabags, crushed eggshells, bread or shredded paper.

Small pieces: the more you mince up their food beforehand, the better. Smaller particles are much easier for them to eat and digest than large particles. As well as adding food in small pieces, small doses of food are also preferred, especially early on, when the number of worms in your farm is still small. If you get the hang of feeding them right, they'll increase in population, and you can add more food each time you open the lid.

Hated foods: don't give them acidic foods such as citrus peelings, acid fruits, onions or garlic. And don't give them too much food, either, especially early on.

Problems

Smells: adding too much food which the worms cannot eat will mean that the uneaten food rots and will smell. If you add too many wet fruit and vegie scraps it will get too wet, so balance things with some drier offerings, such as shredded newspaper.

Pests: if the lid isn't secure, a worm farm can attract cockroaches, ants, rats or mice, so make sure the lid is secure.
Little flies: these can be fungus gnats or 'vinegar flies' and they're attracted to an unbalanced worm farm. A sprinkling of wood ash, lime or dolomite lime will change the pH inside the farm, and the flies may disappear. But also change the balance of what you're putting into the bin, as it's too acid.

The bottom line on worm farms

If space is tight, worm farms are a good idea, and if the kids want one, get one—they're very educational, too. However, they're not as 'dead-easy' as some of the people selling worm farms try to tell you, and they do require a fair bit of work, trial and error, and persistence to get one up and running successfully. But lots of schools and schoolkids manage to do it, so give it a try if the idea appeals.

However, if you have space for either a compost bin or a worm farm, and you're trying to choose between the two, we'd definitely recommend a compost bin. A compost bin should be able to gobble up a much greater amount of scraps—and a much bigger variety of scraps—and is no more work to look after than a worm farm.

If all else fails

It is essential to try not to send too much organic matter to the tip. About 50% of all household waste is compostable material and it causes problems in landfill. If you can't compost it, consider digging a small hole under a shrub about 50cm square and 30cm deep. Dump your household waste and even lawn clippings into it until it is nearly full, then cover it with the soil you dug out. As you dig more holes around the garden, your soil will get better and better.

DIY compost tumbler

Don recently showed viewers on *A Current Affair* how to build your own compost tumbler bin for a little over $60, which compares brilliantly with the more than $200 you'd pay for even the most basic tumble composter bin at the shops. For the full details of how it's done, with all the nuts, bolts, washers, tools needed, contacts, detailed instructions and prices, see the Burke's Backyard website at www.burkesbackyard.com.au

But here's the basics of how we did it, to give you the idea and get you interested. You'll need to be a bit of a home-handyperson to build it, but it didn't take all that long to set it up—just one day. However, it's definitely a two-person job, so get someone practical to help.

You'll need

- an olive barrel with a large screw lid (available from some produce stores, or try Drum Reconditioners or Recyclers in the Yellow Pages)
- 2 x H4 treated pine posts 2.4m long for the mounting frame
- 2 bags concrete, for setting the pine posts securely into the ground
- 1m galvanised 15mm pipe as the axis for the olive barrel to spin on
- 1m 12mm galvanised threaded rod (goes inside the 15mm pipe and, when set up with bushings and nuts, etc holds the olive barrel in place)
- washers and nuts for the threaded rod
- threaded white plastic bushings to help the olive barrel spin smoothly
- spirit level, drill and bits, plus other tools (these are listed at our website)

The design

It's simple. The two treated pine posts are concreted into the ground (far enough apart for your wheelbarrow to be parked in between them with ease). Then the olive barrel is drilled with holes at its exact centre point of balance, and fitted with bushes, and then it's mounted on the galvanised pipe so it spins freely at the right height off the ground so a wheelbarrow slides in underneath with 50mm clearance, for easy loading. The threaded rod which goes through the larger pipe is attached to the mounting posts and holds it all together. Lots of extra air holes are drilled into the barrel to improve aeration of the compost. The beauty of this design is that it's cheap, very good at composting and, best of all, you can wheel a barrow straight under it for easy loading.

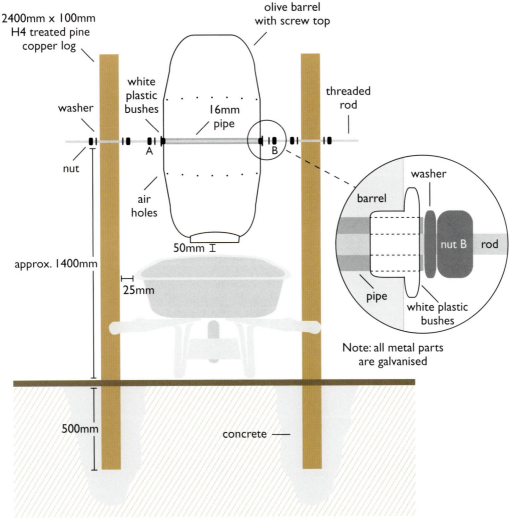

Staying organic

Pots, tubs and troughs

If you don't have much space available, you can grow organic vegetables in containers such as pots, tubs and troughs. All you need is a sunny spot and the time to provide them with the little bit of extra care they'll need. Here's how to get started.

All sorts of vegies can be grown in containers, so if you don't have much space you can still enjoy your fair share of that wonderful, home-grown organic goodness.

Another good reason for growing vegies in pots is that you can get around problems with your garden soil not being all that great for vegie growing. And pots allow you to move plants so they can escape cold snaps in winter, or scorchers in summer.

However, there are some important little basics you need to know which will increase your chances of success. The main thing is that growing vegies in pots is a bit more work than growing them in the ground, and that's because of the need for very regular water and feeding for potted vegies, especially during summer. If you can manage that, the rest is plain sailing.

ABOVE: The rule for potted vegies is simple—choose the biggest pot or container that you can fit into the space available.

Pot basics

Pot size: the rule for potted vegies is simple—choose the biggest pot or container that you can fit into the space available. The more potting mix you have, the happier vegies will be, and the slower the soil will dry out on a hot day. The pot doesn't have to be tall—around 30cm is sufficient but a bit more depth wouldn't hurt. And pot shape doesn't matter much—it can be square, oblong, round or whatever fits the space. However, straight-sided pots are preferable to curved-sided pots. Remember also that tall pots can blow over in the wind, so avoid any over 50cm high.

Pot material: plastic is fine, so are ceramics, terracotta, timber (eg, half wine barrels), stone, concrete, metal or something else that holds potting mix (we've seen vegie gardens grown in old laundry tubs, coppers and aluminium dinghies, and they all seemed to work pretty well). Modern plastic pots are excellent, as they retain soil moisture well, have plenty of drainage holes and are light, an important factor for pots on decks.

Drainage holes: all pots need an adequate number of drainage holes in the bottom, to let water escape freely. At least three drainage holes per pot is ideal, and one hole is often not enough. You might need to get out a drill to create some more holes if

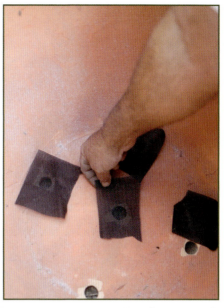

TOP LEFT: If there aren't sufficient holes in your pot, use a drill with a masonry bit to make some more.

TOP RIGHT: A few pieces of fly wire over the holes will prevent potting mix spilling out.

there aren't enough. It's a good idea to place a couple of pieces of flyscreen wire over the holes to stop the potting mix spilling out. If you are improvising a pot from a recycled object, adding drainage holes is extremely important, so remember to get that right.

BELOW: Always put your pots on feet, even if they are in a saucer.

Setting up

Sunny spot: like all vegie gardens in garden beds, your potted vegie garden needs to be in a very sunny spot. A minimum of six hours of direct sunlight is what you need. That's why indoor potted vegie gardens don't work—they don't get enough direct sunshine.

Pot feet: as well as providing pots themselves with drainage holes to let water flow out, sit the pot up on pot feet, so the water drains away. Don't sit pots in dishes which collect water, as it's bad for plant health to have constantly 'wet feet'. If you don't want escaping water to create a mess on your balcony or deck, set up your pot feet inside a dish, but never let the base of the pot itself sit in water (so figure how much water is 'too much' each time you water your pot).

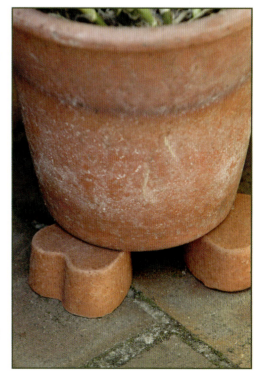

Staying organic

TOP LEFT: Use the best potting mix you can find, look out for the Australian Standard tick to ensure a good quality mix.

TOP RIGHT: Once your vegies are planted, keep them growing rapidly with a soluble or liquid plant food every fortnight.

Potting mix essentials

Use a good quality mix: look for the Australian Standards 'ticks' logo on bags of potting mix. The 'Premium' grade of potting mix contains added slow-release fertiliser that is good for three months' growth. The 'Standard' grade is still a good potting mix, but it contains no added fertiliser. If you want to be a purist organic gardener, the Standard mix allows you to add your own choice of fertiliser, but you must add fertiliser to a Standard mix, or the plants growing in it, from the start.

Don't use garden soil: many garden soils are far too dense to use in pots. Vegies need a light, free-draining soil in which their roots can rapidly grow. So, even though garden soil seems like a money-saver, it's a potted plant killer, usually.

Feeding and watering

Feeding: if you like, you can add extra fertiliser to your potting mix prior to planting, but it's not essential, as top quality modern potting mixes come with slow-release fertilisers already added. However, if you like, you can add a sprinkle of slow-release fertiliser, or a handful of chicken poo, and mix it into your potting mix (exception: don't add extra fertiliser if you're growing root crops such as carrots). Once you have planted your

vegies, keep them growing rapidly with a soluble or liquid plant food every fortnight.

Watering: you'll have to learn what your potted vegies like, but be prepared to water pots daily in summer. Naturally enough, in cooler winter weather they might not need watering so often, but as a general rule, all potted vegies will need more regular watering than vegies grown in garden beds.

What you can grow

Leafy vegies: these are probably the best choices for pots and troughs, and they include all the salad greens (such as lettuce, radicchio, rocket, endive, English spinach, silver beet, etc) and the Asian greens (such as Chinese cabbage, Chinese chard, Chinese broccoli and various others). The Asian greens are very fast-growing and more compact, so if you want to grow a cabbage in a container, choose a fast-growing Chinese cabbage over a traditional, big European-style Savoy cabbage, for example.

ABOVE: Asian greens grow very quickly in pots.

Root crops: carrots are easy enough to grow in containers of at least 30cm depth, so too beetroot, but slow-growing parsnips prefer very cold soil and aren't such a great choice. Potatoes can be grown in tall pots.

Mini vegies: vegies such as cauliflowers, beetroot, pumpkins, carrots and beans are now available as 'mini vegies' which are much smaller plants than the full-size ones, and these are great choices for containers. Vegies such as beans and peas come in both 'climbing' and 'bush' plants, and the 'bush' varieties are the ones to go for with pots.

Tomatoes: bush cherry tomatoes are the ideal choice for pots and other containers. Unfortunately, the tall, staking types of tomatoes aren't a good choice for pots.

Chillies: while chilli plants vary in size depending on the variety, these can make very good potted plants.

Herbs: see our chapter on growing herbs for the details, but we prefer to grow most of our herbs in pots.

ABOVE: Herbs can be grown in pots in the tiniest of spaces.

Shallots/spring onions: these are a great choice for pots, as they can be harvested one by one, as needed in the kitchen. They don't take up much space in the pot itself, either, so you have room for other vegies beside them.

Lemon grass: this is a bit like shallots and spring onions in that lemon grass grows well in a pot and can provide a very handy stalk of flavour when needed, one at a time.

Poor choices

Any plants which grow tall, and especially those which need staking, are not great choices for pots, unless you have a large pot and a solid wall or other structure behind the pot, which you can tie the plant to. So, tall tomatoes aren't a great choice for pots. Capsicum plants, which can become heavy with fruit and need staking, aren't that terrific, either. Same problem with potted eggplant. Most pumpkins and melons sprawl too widely to be suitable for pots and we don't recommend them for corn either.

Climbing plants such as some beans, passionfruit, grapes etc are very susceptible to the soil drying out in summer, and rarely do well in pots, especially during summer scorchers.

Special cases

Potted fruit trees

Unlike most vegies, which will spend only a couple of months in your potting mix, fruit trees are there for the long haul, so they need a different soil mix and a different feeding program.

Potting mix: modern potting mixes don't contain any soil at all, and so over time they break down and as this happens the potting mix slumps lower and lower in the pot. As fruit trees will spend years in their pot, you can reduce this problem by making a special potting mix. Combine a top quality potting mix 50:50 with washed coarse sand. The sand adds body to the mix, improves drainage and, most importantly, doesn't break down.

Fertiliser: while various fruit trees require different amounts of food, many of them, notably the most popular choice—citrus—thrive on regular feeds. So, the idea with potted citrus is to lightly feed them every four to six weeks, which is much more often than you'd feed a citrus tree growing in a garden bed. Give them a handful of Dynamic Lifter, or a liquid food formulated for fruit and flowers once a month in summer, once every six weeks

BOTTOM LEFT: Citrus are a good choice if you want to grow fruit in pots but they will need regular fertilising to do well.

BOTTOM RIGHT: Fruit trees in pots benefit from being planted in a 50:50 mix of top quality potting mix and washed coarse sand.

in winter. Alternatively, apply slow-release fertiliser formulated for citrus, and follow the directions on the packet.

Best fruit trees for pots: all the new 'dwarf' varieties of fruit trees now storming the market are the ones to grow in pots. You get full-size fruit, and much smaller plants. Other good choices for pots include: cumquats, a naturally small-growing citrus; figs, which seem to fruit better with cramped roots; and the kaffir lime, which has unusual and aromatic 'waisted' leaves that provide a lot of flavour in Thai cooking. A word of warning with the kaffir lime: it's very thorny and shouldn't be placed anywhere that people will brush past as they pass by.

Potatoes

Potatoes are a special case because of the way they grow. As the plants grow, you hill up around the base of the plant with soil, straw, compost, potting mix or whatever works for you, to prevent the developing potatoes located at the base of the plant being exposed to sunlight.

Lots of people grow potatoes in a wire cage of potting mix and straw and keep on adding a soil/straw mix as the plants grow. Others do it in a circle of tyres (this isn't the best look for a stylish balcony, of course) but it works. However, the bottom line is that if you're determined to grow potatoes in a pot you can, and lots of people do it very successfully.

BELOW: With regular watering, strawberries thrive in pots.

Strawberries

We've seen some excellent strawberry plants grown in pots, and they're a credit to their owner's ability with a watering can. However, they are a lot of work and need a very steady supply of water and fertiliser to keep on cropping well. Strawberries can look fantastic when grown in a hanging basket, and these are even more thirsty than ordinary pots. But lots of people manage to do it very well! So, if you want to take on a strawberry in a pot or basket, have a go, and good luck. And if you succeed—well done, top effort!

Kids in the garden

Growing their own delicious fruits and vegies is the best way to get children interested in gardening. Start off by planting some of their favourite foods, and if you have space, give them their own patch to look after, too.

Yummy favourites

Our best tip is to let the kids grow what they want to grow, and that will usually be their favourite foods. Very popular choices that are great plants for beginners to start with include:
- beans *
- carrots *
- corn *
- lettuce
- mandarins and other citrus
- peas *
- potatoes
- pumpkin *
- strawberries
- watermelon *
- zucchini *

* all of these are also good from seed

Add some flowers

While vegie-growing might be what started the kids off on gardening, adding in some flowers is a good idea because they make the vegie garden look prettier, and they give kids the chance to learn about flowers, bees and other garden insects. If you or the kids aren't sure what to grow, here are some good flowers to try.

- Marigolds are a great choice for vegie patches. They can be planted and grown for many months, seedlings are cheap and readily available at garden centres, and they won't spread and take over the vegie beds, which some other flowers (such as petunias) can tend to do.
- Pansies are a good choice during the cooler months, when not a lot of annual flowers are available. They come in a huge range of colours, so let the kids pick the pansies in their favourite colour for their own patch.
- Sunflowers are much taller plants than marigolds—and all vegies for that matter—so they should be planted at the back of the bed, but they are a fantastic choice that will delight children. As they're best grown from seed, sunflowers are also very educational, as well as being tall, cheerful and exciting!
- Ask your local garden centre what flowers they recommend as well, as they'll have the local knowledge of what grows well in your area.

Collect bugs

While your children will learn a packet about vegies, soils, worms, seeds, plants and gardening in general, the educational benefits of gardening don't stop there. They can learn all about nature and wildlife at the same time, but it is advisable to provide plenty of adult supervision early on, so you prevent your young biologists making contact with spiders, wasps and anything else worth avoiding.

One simple way to get them started is to collect bugs in a glass jar, with air holes punched in the lid to keep the insect alive. Get out some reference books or start surfing the net and see if you can identify which bug it is. Once he or she knows the bug's name (Tip: maybe a schoolteacher or the local garden centre staff can help?) your child can then make it a little project to learn a bit more about the bug: what it eats, how it lives, etc.

Keeping chooks

The medical truth is that kids who have a pet such as a dog are significantly less likely to develop allergies. It seems that excessive cleanliness causes more allergies. A somewhat dirty pet seems to prime kids' immune systems to fight off bugs, etc leading to fewer allergies throughout life. So chooks probably help in this way, too.

I can still remember as a five-year-old the first time I went across the road to Mr Bagley's place. He was a lovely man who had time for us neighbourhood kids. But best of all he had chooks. I remember the smell of the pollard and cornmeal that he mixed with water to feed them. I remember the stale bread and the outer leaves off the lettuce from Mr Bagley's vegie garden that I was allowed to feed to the chooks.

I remember how excited and grateful the chooks were. I vividly remember all the smells: the wet dirt, the chook poo, the perfume from the blossoms on the citrus trees in the chook yard. Most of all I remember carrying some eggs home for my breakfast.

I remember that we were never allowed to keep chooks at our place. Nor dogs or cats. The social truth is that your kids will remember if you didn't let them have pets.

Chooks:
- Eat kitchen scraps
- Provide fresh eggs
- Teach the kids about nature and responsibility
- Are fascinating to watch
- Provide useful garden manure

Do remember that the food scraps go to the chooks then they re-emerge as eggs and poo. The poo fertilises the vegie garden which feeds you and the bits of the garden left over go back to the chooks to start the whole cycle again.

Homegrown eggs taste better and, if you feed the chooks scraps, have a deep orange yolks. If you are really keen you may be able to keep a rooster (check with your local council). Then you can have baby chickens and the kids learn about the chooks and the bees. Normal laying hens do not need a rooster to produce eggs. They just start laying at puberty (around 28 weeks of age). It is worth noting that unfertilised eggs don't go rotten—ie, smell of rotten egg gas. The really rotten ones are dead fertilised eggs.

The most popular breed

ISA Browns: Most people seem to get ISA Browns which are a brownish/white colour, being a hybrid between a Rhode Island Red and a Rhode Island White. They lay slightly more eggs per year than other specially bred egg layers, but not enough to make a difference for home production. (See photo page 165)

Overall, I don't recommend ISA Browns. They are more highly strung than other egg-laying chooks and can tend to feather-pluck or vent pluck other chooks. The vent plucking produces a fair amount of bleeding and it can be hard to identify the plucker. Some farmers say to hang up some raw liver in an onion bag. The chooks eat this and often stop plucking.

ISA Browns were developed for the commercial egg laying industry. They lay around 305 eggs per year. There is some evidence that their huge egg output leads to poorer nutritional quality of the egg contents.

They tend to be a bit uptight, making them less suitable for people who want to chill out while they watch the chooks and also less suitable for kids who want to cuddle the chooks.

Better choices

Specialised layer chooks have been selected over the last century for very high egg production of around 280 to 300 eggs per year. They have been selected not to go broody, or to do it very rarely. They just lay an egg at least five days out of seven. This is what we have all grown to expect.

The female chooks usually only produce at this high level for about two years, after which production drops off dramatically. Commercially, the chickens are usually disposed of after about two years of laying and are replaced by younger birds.

In backyards, we all tend to include our hens as part of the family...well certainly my family does. But after three years of age the hens don't lay much any more. Some do lay some eggs, but many hardly lay at all. So they are no longer earning their keep. My family has never killed off our old chooks. We just let them live out their lives scratching for worms and enjoying their social order. Chooks can live on to 10 years of age or more, although the average lifespan is probably around six or seven years. Thus, every two or three years you need to buy a few more chooks. So let's crunch some numbers.

Layer hens produce about five eggs a week for two years, although they do stop laying during their annual winter moult. If you buy three hens you get 15 eggs per week. If this is enough, you start with three hens. After two years of laying you need, say, two more to take up the slack in reduced egg production. After another two years you need two more, which means that after four years you have seven chooks, at least three of which don't lay much any more. Given that some will eventually die of old age, the number of chooks should stabilise at around seven chooks (as you regularly purchase two more each two years).

The other option is to dispose of and replace the older hens as they cease laying, thus allowing you to maintain a constant number of three laying hens and an output of 15 eggs per week.

There is some merit in this option as introducing young pullets to your original three older girls is not without risks. Chooks have a rigid pecking order and this involves bullying. The new little girls could be badly beaten up by the old girls, so they may need to be housed separately until they are fully grown (ie, laying eggs at 21 weeks or so).

Types of chooks

Broadly there are four types of chooks:
1. Purebred egg layers
2. Crossbred egg layers
3. Meat chooks
4. Purebred ornamental chooks.

The same breed name can occur in all four types, thus you can get a White Leghorn variety of purebred egg layer, crossbred egg layer, meat chook or ornamental (exhibition) chook.

1. Purebred egg layers—mostly these consist of three breeds:
- The White Leghorn (pronounced Leg-rn): neither the 'o' nor the 'h' is pronounced as this is old name for the port of Livorno in Italy where the breed came from)
- The Rhode Island Red
- The Australorp (the Australian variety of the Black Orpington) that is white, red or black

There are many other purebred chooks that lay a lot of eggs, but none lay anywhere near as many eggs as the above three breeds.

Overall, the White Leghorns lay the most eggs, laying perhaps up to 180 or so eggs per year. The Reds and Blacks lay about 170 but all of these numbers vary in different lines of each breed and also due to different management regimes.

The best egg-laying variety for backyards is the Australorp. These are docile, placid chooks that lay lots of eggs, but don't attack each other, people collecting eggs or children.

It is said by some experts that over three years the purebred layers will lay more eggs than the crossbred varieties.

2. Crossbred egg layers—these come in 4 varieties
- The ISA Brown (a cross between a Rhode Island Red and a Rhode Island White (see photo page 165)
- The White Leghorn Cross (see photo page 164)
- The Rhode Island Red Cross (see pic page 164)
- The Australorp (black) cross (see pic page 164)

The ISA Browns lay up to about 305 eggs per year, and the others lay up to about 295 eggs per year. Ten eggs per year is not a great difference.

The standout again for backyards is the black Australorp cross. It is very placid, strutting around like a dowager empress. Always pleased to see you, they seem to regard aggression in any form as unseemly. It is said that the crossbreds' egg production in the third year is not as good as the purebreds' (see facing page).

3. Meat chooks

These are not usually raised in backyards any more since you have to chop off their heads, hang them up to bleed, then pluck and disembowel them prior to cooking. The birds can be any colour, but are usually white or greyish. They are eaten at about 8–10 weeks of age. Yes, they really do grow that fast. But I could never bring myself to kill them.

4. Purebred ornamental chooks

These varieties are bred by hobbyists for exhibition purposes and they include: White Leghorns, Rhode Island Reds, Australorps, various bantams, game fowls (fighting chooks) and weird breeds like Silkies and Frizzles.

These are tremendous fun to breed and show, but they are not the egg-laying machines that the ones above are. For instance, some Rhode Island Reds would only lay 7–10 eggs per year.

Many ornamental breeds are spectacularly beautiful, but my recommendation is probably either the silky variety (see pic page 165) or perhaps a Bantam Frizzle (see pic page 166). Neither can fly, so they can't escape. The Silkies in particular are small, docile, friendly chooks—possibly the best chook in the world for kids. They lay up to 100 smallish eggs per year and come in white, buff, black, blue and a few other colours. They go broody and make excellent foster mums for the other chooks' eggs and chickens.

Bantam Frizzles have more spiky than fluffy feathers and they too have difficulty flying. They come in a similar colour range to Silkies. They are not quite as gentle as Silkies nor do they lay as many eggs.

If you select Silkies, you need at least eight to ten to equal the egg output of three crossbreds.

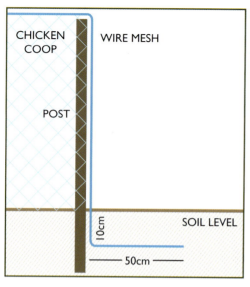

Housing

You should try for two square metres of floor area for each bird, that is 2m x 1m. So for three chooks you need six square metres and for seven chooks you need 14 square metres, or roughly 5m x 3m. Ideally about half of the area is enclosed in rainproof cladding (eg, corrugated iron) and the other half is just chook mesh. Be sure to mesh the top as foxes can climb in and eat the chooks. To fox proof the sides, bury the mesh into the ground about 10cm down and bend it 50cm out from the walls. See diagram, left, for how to fox-proof a chook house.

If you have very little space, you could drop down to one square metre per chook. So seven chooks would need seven square metres or about 2m x 3.5m.

Feeding

Feed your chooks egg layer pellets plus kitchen scraps and water and try to place their pen in a sunny area. Most chooks like to roost on wooden or pipe perching about 2m off the ground in the sheltered section of the pen. So, construct a ladder of, say, four roosting perches separated by 40cm at about 45 degrees to the ground. Four laying boxes should suffice for your three or four regular layers.

What to get

Laying chooks

In our opinion, the following cross-bred chooks make the best backyard laying chooks. These crossbreds are far more easily available than the purebreds.

Black Australorp Cross

(Our No. 1 backyard laying chook)

Eggs per year: 295.
Personality: Very friendly, docile, cheerful and inquisitive. Great with kids.
Appearance: An attractive round, black chook with the odd tinge of red. Quite robust.

White Leghorn Cross

Eggs per year: 295.
Personality: Somewhat wary and standoffish, but not aggressive.
Appearance: Plain white, with a bright red comb and wattles.

Rhode Island Red Cross

Eggs per year: 295.
Personality: Calm, friendly, although cocks sometimes fight. Can fly so needs to be kept in an enclosure.
Appearance: A dark red, strong-looking chook with the odd black feather, with yellow legs and feet.

Crossbred layers

ISA Brown

Eggs per year: 305 (the most productive layer).
Personality: Can be highly-strung and can be aggressive towards other chooks.
Appearance: An orangey-red colour with some whitish feathers.

Purebred ornamental chooks

These are fundamentally different from laying chooks in that they have been bred for their appearance (ie, to look pretty and win at shows) NOT for egg production. There are hundreds of ornamental breeds and colours you could try, so it really comes down to personal preference, but here are a few of our favourites.

Silkie
(Our No. 1 ornamental chook)

Eggs per year: Varies, up to 100.
Personality: Very placid and calm, trusting, can't fly, fantastic with kids.
Appearance: Cute. Fluffy all over, available in many colours.

Frizzle Bantam

Eggs per year: Varies, under 90.
Personality: Friendly, cute, reasonably relaxed.
Appearance: Curly feathers all over, available in many colours

Pekin Bantam

Eggs per year: Varies, some produce a low quantity of small eggs.
Personality: A lovely relaxed and friendly chook. Good with people.
Appearance: A round, cuddly ball. Nice fluffy, feather duster bum, short legs with feathery feet, lots of colours.

Silver Spangled Hamburg

Eggs per year: Varies, up to 200.
Personality: Friendly, curious, sprightly.
Appearance: White with black spots all over. Very pretty.

Orpingtons

Eggs per year: Varies, up to 200.
Personality: Friendly, relaxed (easily go broody).
Appearance: Large (3–4kg), plump-looking, available in many colours.

Transylvanian Naked Neck

Eggs per year: Varies, up to 120.
Personality: Fairly easy going, calm.
Appearance: No feathers on the neck, a bit like a vulture. Available in many colours.

Houdan and Polish

Eggs per year: varies.
Personality: Generally placid.
Appearance: Both these breeds have a huge feathery crown on the head. Quite spectacular.

Araucana

Eggs per year: Varies. Not huge layers but they lay light blue eggs!
Personality: Hens friendly, roosters can be aggressive towards people.
Appearance: Small, soft greyish lavender blue colour, also available in other colours.

Cochin

Eggs per year: Varies; generally considered to be good layers.
Personality: Relaxed, placid, friendly.
Appearance: Large, round, attractive chook with feathery feet. Lots of colours to choose from.

Barnevelder

Eggs per year: Varies. Generally considered very good layers.
Personality: Fairly placid, robust.
Appearance: Handsome, attractive, bold-looking chook, glossy feathers.

Wyandotte or Wyandotte Bantam

Eggs per year: Varies.
Personality: Friendly, placid, good with kids (esp the bantams).
Appearance: An attractive, round chook available in many colours, the laced pattern (pictured) is popular.

Brama Bantam

Eggs per year: Varies.
Personality: Placid, generally relaxed.
Appearance: Large for a bantam, high tails, feathery feet, available in many colours with interesting feather patterns.

Game (meat) chooks

Game chooks are big, heavy birds bred primarily for eating, so laying is not a priority. All of the game fowl have their origins in fighting birds. That having been said, many are very handsome and can have fun personalities that make them worth a try.

Malay Game

Eggs per year: Varies, but not many.
Personality: Self-confident, smart. Will fight with other chooks, so best kept in numbers under three.
Appearance: Heavy, tall, small combs, feathers sit sleekly on their bodies.

Where to buy chooks

Many chook breeds can be hard to find, here's a few places to try:
- For suppliers in your area, look under 'Poultry Suppliers and Dealers' in the Yellow Pages. The Trading Post also regularly lists suppliers.
- Semi-rural produce stores sometimes sell them or know of locals who do.
- When you're driving through a rural area, keep your eyes peeled and if you see a sign on the side of the road saying: "Crossbred pullets for sale", pull over.
- Another good tip is to buy a copy of *Australasian Poultry Magazine*, your newsagent can order a copy for you, or call (03) 5792 4000 to subscribe.
- All of the companies listed in the 'Try Before You Buy' paragraph below sell chooks. Websites and contact details follow for Vic, Qld and NSW.
- Barter and Sons Chooks in Sydney sells a range of laying chooks; ph: (02) 4773 3222.
- Brian Larkin, Tahmoor, NSW supplies to the public; ph: (02) 4681 9722.
- For rare breeds, you can simply Google the name of the rare breed you're looking for (with the 'pages from Australia' box checked) or the websites listed below are also a good starting point:
- www.backyardpoultry.com
- www.rarepoultry.net

Try before you buy

If you're not sure about committing to keeping chooks, there are several companies that allow you to rent a coop and chooks to try at your place for 6 weeks or so. If you like them, you keep them, if you don't you can send them back. They also sell coops and chickens if you're ready to commit straight away.
Brisbane: City Chicks; (07) 3300 6801, www.citychicks.com.au
Melbourne: Book a Chook; 0438 540 664, www.bookachook.com
Sydney: Rent-a-chook; 0409 246 651, www.rentachook.com.au

Real people
who've done it themselves

Gardening in small spaces

In their small inner-city backyard, Pam and Jamie have created a pretty little potager-style vegie garden filled with flowers and lots of herbs and vegies. They both love to cook, and there's always something home-grown being added to the pot.

OPPOSITE: Broad beans, snow peas, cabbages, spinach and herbs galore.

BELOW: The garden in 1991, when Pam and Jamie first moved in, and in 2008.

Just a few kilometres from the centre of Sydney, Pam and Jamie are growing herbs, vegies and flowers galore in their little backyard. And we mean 'little'—it's only nine metres long and a bit over seven metres wide. But that small space isn't a problem for them—they just really pack in the plants wherever they can find a space.

When they first bought the property in the early 1990s, Pam and Jamie wanted to start up a kitchen garden, and the previous owners, Jim and Angela, a Greek couple, had given them a great head start. They had planted two olive trees, and both of them are still growing beautifully all these years later.

Neither Jamie nor Pam had done much gardening before they moved in, so this is their first garden. "And I reckon it's going to be our last garden too," says Jamie with a laugh. "We're rusted onto Marrickville now and we can't imagine ever moving anywhere else. We love it here."

Dumb things

Jamie happily quotes songwriter Paul Kelly and says, as a gardener: "I've done all the dumb things. At first I had plants in the wrong spot, and they died. And I put tall plants in front of short ones, crammed too many plants into small spaces, and just tried to grow things that didn't work and would never work here. But I had my early successes too, as well as some failures, and as the years have gone by I've learned a lot more about gardening. I love it. I love growing herbs and crops of vegies, and using crops I have grown myself in my cooking."

The big change in the garden is due to Pam. "She came home one day with a photo from a magazine in her hand and said 'I want that'. It was quite a simple backyard layout: a shed at the back, with a pathway leading straight out to the shed, and with little side pathways reaching out to the edges. There was no lawn. Apart from the pathways, the whole area was planted out with herbs, vegies and flowers. And so I ripped up the lawn and a

RIGHT: This picture from a magazine provided inspiration for the garden's design.

LEFT: The garden at Christmas last year. It's a potager-style garden, a mix of flowers and vegies in the same beds.

paving company did the rest of the work, the hard yakka. Getting rid of the lawn and turning the whole backyard into a potager garden was the best thing we have ever done here," says Jamie.

Pam's visitors

Pam is a botanical illustrator (they're her garden plan illustrations in this book) and she works from home. Her studio overlooks the garden and she loves seeing what comes and goes through the garden during the day. "A few years ago Jamie gave me a small pair of binoculars, and I keep them next to my desk. Whenever I see a bird sitting on the clothesline or hopping around in a grevillea or down on the ground, I whip out the binoculars and check out who's visiting. As well as the usual wattlebirds, willy wagtails, blue wrens, kookaburras, magpies and New Holland honeyeaters that we see here all the time, we've had some unusual birds here in our little inner-city garden, such as black-faced cuckoo shrikes, sacred kingfishers and spotted pardalotes—they're really pretty. We do have some native plants here, such as

BELOW: Bulbuls and other birds are regular visitors to the city oasis.

177

Real people

grevilleas, but I think our birdbaths are important for attracting birds to the garden, too."

"Pam has a fantastic eye for spotting problems in the garden," says Jamie. "She often says 'have you noticed that's something's eating the silver beet?' (or whatever) and I usually haven't. I do most of the gardening here, I'm the one who gets dirt under my nails, but Pam and I decide together what we're going to grow, and she keeps a really close eye on how everything is going and has saved countless plants from trouble. I suppose it's her artist's training, but she notices everything going on out there. And the walls inside our house are filled with Pam's lovely paintings and drawings of things from our garden, too."

RIGHT: Pam's watercolour illustration of the garden shows the basic layout of the paths, but every year the planting plan changes.

LEFT: Handy herb pots make it easy to dash outside while cooking, snip off a few leaves and pop them in the pan a few seconds later.

Herb mixture

"We like to grow a mixture of herbs, vegies and flowers here. I love food plants, and so we're always growing them," says Jamie. "I'm often growing new plants that I haven't tried before. But I find herbs are the best value plants, per square inch, as far as food flavour goes. I use fresh herbs all the time in cooking, and it's great to just dash out the back door, snip off some parsley or chives or thyme or whatever I need, and pop it in the pot a few seconds later. Herbs don't take up much space, and the freshly cut herbs definitely taste better than shop-bought ones which might have been cut a day or two before you get to buy them."

Jamie has plenty of herbs growing here: parsley, sage, rosemary, thyme, oregano, mint, marjoram, basil, tarragon, chives, dill and coriander. And there's a beautiful curry-leaf tree (*Murraya koenigii*) growing in a large pot to add flavour to his curries. "One of the tricks with herbs is to keep on picking and trimming them. Herbs can get a bit straggly if you never pick any leaves, so even if you don't need herbs for cooking, it's still a good idea to snip them back regularly to make them a bit more dense and bushy."

BELOW: The striking curry-leaf tree does well in a pot and adds some authentic aromas to curry night.

Vegie goodness

"My favourite crop here is salad greens," says Jamie. "We use them all the time. As well as lettuce, we grow rocket, English spinach and mesclun mixed salad leaves almost all through the year. The only time I don't bother growing them is the hottest part of summer—they don't do so well then."

Apart from his salad greens and his fruit trees (lime, lemon, cumquat, olives), last year Jamie grew little crops of the following vegies: beetroot, broad beans, broccoli, Brussels sprouts, bok choy, carrots, choy sum, English spinach, garlic, green beans, parsnips, potatoes, radishes, shallots, snow peas, strawberries, tomatoes, turnips and wombok (Chinese cabbage). "As always, I had my successes and failures," says Jamie with a laugh. "The Brussels sprouts were hopeless. Plants looked great, but dud sprouts. Don't know what I did wrong there! And while the cherry tomatoes were fantastic, I lost a couple of Roma tomato plants to a sudden mystery disease. That was a real shame. But the broad beans were the absolute stars last year, really delicious. Some of the carrots were a bit hilarious to look at, but they tasted great.

OPPOSITE: 'Blue Lake' beans climb up a cone of willow.

LEFT: Chinese cabbage, baby turnips, salad greens and shallots all crowd into the one garden bed.

The parsnips were the sweetest, nicest, tenderest parsnips I've ever eaten. And the spuds weren't half-bad either!"

Going organic

"I guess you could call me an organic gardener," says Jamie. "As for fertilisers I've always used chicken manure, compost and dolomite lime for preparing the garden beds. And I always mix up a 50:50 blend of Seasol and Nitrosol in a watering can and apply that once plants are growing well—it's magic on all the leafy greens, especially.

"I don't like using any toxic sprays on something that we'll eat later on, but I do occasionally use organic sprays, such as Dipel or Success to control caterpillars, and Pestoil to control citrus leafminer, aphids and scale insects. And my home-made Vegemite powered fruit fly trap gets a lot of customers, too!

"I'd say that the main thing about gardening organically is that every year your soil gets better. The manure, compost and mulch feeds the soil, and the worms love it. The soil here is much better, richer and more fertile than it was 10 years ago."

BOTTOM LEFT: Beautiful and tasty home-grown snow peas.

BOTTOM RIGHT: The broad beans were the absolute stars last year, really delicious.

Tidy compost

Hidden behind a tidy little hedge of clipped murraya plants is Jamie's composting set-up, which produces all the compost he needs for his garden. Jamie has two bins here—a bigger plastic tumbler-style bin and the original, smaller black plastic bin which he started with, and which never worked that well. The good news is there are no dodgy smells or messes here—it's all pretty tidy.

"I love my tumbler bin," says Jamie. "It holds a lot more than you might imagine, and if you remember to give it a spin once every weekend, everything breaks down pretty quickly."

Why two bins, then? "Oh, you need two compost bins because eventually the big tumbler bin will fill up, and it then needs a couple of months for everything to break down completely and become nice, sweet-smelling compost. While I'm waiting for that to happen, we start adding kitchen scraps and garden clippings, etc to the old back-up bin. I'm always tossing old potting mix into the backup bin, too, so it has its handy uses, even if it's not as good as the tumbler."

In their kitchen, Jamie and Pam take turns cooking and both are keen cooks, so they produce a lot of fruit and vegie scraps. Pam says: "We have three bins set up under the sink. One is for garbage headed for the tip, another is for paper, bottles and plastics for recycling, and the third one is for all the vegie and fruit scraps destined for the compost bin. It all works pretty well."

"While in theory you can compost anything that was once a living thing, it's a really good idea to keep as many seeds out of your compost bins as possible," says Jamie. "Seeds don't break down so well in a tumbler bin, as it never gets hot enough inside the bin, and in the first couple of years when I spread out my compost I had hundreds of tomato seedlings coming up! So, these days, we just compost peelings and offcuts, but try to separate out as many seeds as possible. Doing that has made the compost much better to work with."

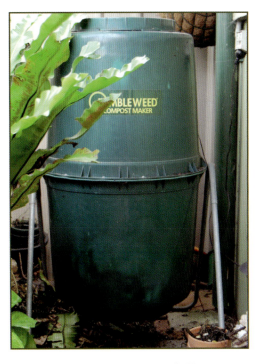

ABOVE: Jamie loves his compost tumbler as it doesn't smell and is small enough to be hidden from view discretely at the back of the garden, behind a hedge.

Jamie's tips

Judging by his garden Jamie seems to have learned a few things over the years, so what are his tips for people starting out?

"Get into the organic way of gardening right from the start. I didn't realise it when I was beginning, but now I know that I was starting up a soil improvement program. It's amazing how much the soil has improved over the years, just through using mulch, manure and compost. The soil here really does get better every year.

"And just get in there and have a go. Grow what you like to eat. Vegies are a fair bit of work compared to most other plants, so don't take on too much if you don't have the time to look after them. And if you make a mistake or a crop fails, don't worry about that at all. That still happens here occasionally—it's all just part of being a backyard farmer!

"We love looking after the garden together. I might be the one covered in dirt, but Pam uses the garden all the time, harvests what she wants, makes suggestions about what to grow next, spots trouble brewing—and she came up with the whole garden design in the first place. And that's what is so good about the garden now. It's a simple layout that looks good and works really well for us." And if you want read more about their garden, check out Jamie's gardening blog at www.gardenamateur.blogspot.com

OPPOSITE: Growing things organically means you'll always have some failures, but nothing beats a basketful of your successes!

LEFT: In summer a cheery blend of salvias, zinnias and marigolds teams with salad greens, parsley borders and chives to create a colourful scene.

An organic country garden

In a suburban-sized block in the Southern Highlands of NSW, Jonathan and Maria's organic Garden of Eden is dripping with late summer fruit and vegetables.

The highly productive garden yields so much produce that friends and neighbours regularly come home to find a colourful bounty of surplus produce abandoned at their front doorsteps.

Incredibly, this organic oasis, fringed with natives, is only three years old. When Jonathan and Maria bought the place there was just a small turn-of-the-century house sitting at the far end of a flat, lawn-covered quarter-acre block. The only trees were a couple of old apples in desperate need of a good prune and some TLC.

The dream

Jonathan (a geophysicist, scientist and teacher) was aching to build a permaculture garden and was delighted with the potential the block offered. "It's blessed with fantastic soils at the base of Mount Gibraltar, which is an old volcano, and from there you get lots of iron-rich, magnesium-rich felsic soils and great rainfall. So you've got two really good factors contributing to success in this area," says Jonathan.

With one daughter already on the ground and hopes for another child to follow soon, both Jonathan and Maria were keen to build a garden in which two-year-old Isabella could watch, touch and eat the produce and witness organic practices first hand.

Maria and Jonathan met in Byron Bay 13 years ago. Jonathan

> "It's important to me that the kids know where the food is coming from and why it's on the table," says Maria.

was raised in Sydney and Canberra but Maria came from a beautiful alpine village high in the Austrian Tyrols, not far from the Italian border. After a few years of toing and froing between Australia and Austria (incorporating a traditional Austrian wedding along the way and the birth of Isabella), Maria and Jonathan put down roots in Mittagong in 2005. An impossibly blond son, Victor, arrived soon after.

Within weeks of moving in, Jonathan already had most of the garden mapped out in his head—a permaculture vision that

would see every square inch of the block used organically. Every part would serve a purpose. Says Jonathan: "I've always loved the concept of permaculture, the permanent agriculture, the cycling through. It's like this big machine moving and all you have to do is just go in occasionally and oil all the cogs. It's a self-perpetuating system, all driven by the sun, the recycling of nitrogen, carbon and oxygen—and that's what I like a lot."

A splendid vision, but a few basics had to be covered first.

Steps one and two, sun and soil

Jonathan says: "I grew up in Sydney in a house that was south-facing. It hardly ever got any sun and I struggled with growing vegies there. Now we've got lovely, lovely exposed north-facing sun, which is the key driver for any system."

Sun, tick!

Jonathan's next mission was soil preparation and, as a scientist, he knew that getting that right was vital and would be the foundation for years of successful crops. He says: "For the first two and a half years the soil profile needed to be improved, so whatever we grew was grown for a purpose, like legumes to nitrify the soil and to build in organic matter. We grew a few quick-growing leafy greens, but the primary focus was the soil. We improved it further by adding green manure and chicken manure, by composting and just—layer after layer—letting it grow down. Now it's fantastic."

Soil, tick!

A place for everything

As the soil renovation process began, Jonathan put in a chicken coop adjacent to the vegetable patch and planted a couple of citrus trees nearby. He also fenced off a central area in which to put in a pond plus some stone fruit trees. The fence itself, while very practical in keeping the kids safe from the pond, also provided a structure

on which to grow a few grapes, raspberries and blackberries. It also gave the chooks an additional area in which to frolic and fertilise during the day, keeping them safe from the jaws of a new Jack Russell Terrier puppy called Arthur who now completes the family unit.

Pathways and layout

Crushed granite pathways also went in, creating easy access to all areas and giving the garden a lovely, meandering feel. Says Jonathan: "I just like the crushed granite, it's durable. I like the colour of it set against the eucalypts. You can have a fire on it or have a whole heap of rubbish then just rake it over and it still looks good."

The house also began a transformation with an extension to accommodate the growing family. But why stop there? Jonathan also put in a cubby house and sandpit for the kids, a shed for his tools and a potting shed to raise his seedlings.

The pond

The pond was built using a butyl rubber liner, with cleverly placed rocks and plants to disguise the bottom and edges. Within a few months it looked natural and beautiful. "You could say aesthetics were involved in its design but it's more functional. It is a habitat, an aqua-cultural hub for the garden," says Jonathan. "It lends itself to a permaculture system. Fruit trees grow near it and the chickens can have access to it to drink. There are two species of frog there and there's a blue tongue lizard, and it's another habitat for flora and fauna, which is the whole point—to create multiple habitats for multiple predators to predate on pests to reduce the number of pests in the organic garden, thereby not requiring any pesticides—that's the aim."

Function aside, it is gorgeous and Isabella and Victor simply adore it, mostly because of one very clever addition by Jonathan:

"I built a walkway into the pond which is a folly but it's an opportunity for the kids to have a look. It's not there to generate produce, it's an aesthetic addition just for interest and for the kids. It overhangs by a couple of metres so you can actually go into the pond and have a look." The pond is also used as part of an aquaponics system that Jonathan installed.

Natives are an organic gardener's best friend

Jonathan and Maria also wanted trees, *lots* of trees. "I love native gardens and I really wanted to spoil myself with native plants, like the Tasmanian blue gum over there. I mean, who would plant that in their garden? What kind of fool would do that? The thing grows to 40m and I've got three of them!" says Jonathan.

Jonathan decided early on to take a 'more is more' approach to the native component of the garden and to do his bit for reducing the family's carbon footprint. "I planted a thousand plants on this block, a quarter-acre block," says Jonathan. "I went up to Wariapendi Nursery, it's a fantastic native nursery up here.

"But I also love the vegetable garden, just that synergy and how you create an environment where they're working. The natives love a prune, just keeping them tidy, not tidy in the sense of a formal garden but keeping them controlled for a purpose. They serve a function as everything in a garden should do and their function is to shade, create privacy and create habitat for predators. Aesthetically it looks nice so there are lots of reasons for the mass-planting of natives, which I love."

The kids

Maria, although sharing Jonathan's passion for a permaculture lifestyle, has also been a strong defender of land rights for the kids. She insisted on the sandpit and a patch of grass for the kids to play on. She says: "They need to be able to do cartwheels and that sort of thing." Jonathan has recently added to the kid's zone by building a little ladder into the apple trees and running a plank between the two. The kids adore it. Simple additions like a sandpit or a ladder on a tree give enormous pleasure to children and are easy to remove when they get older.

Jonathan says: "I find winter is a much more productive time. The conditions are softer, there are fewer pests and better conditions to work in. And all your Asian greens such as bok choy and choy sum come up so quickly."

A by-product of the house extension was the courtyard area the additions created. Says Jonathan: "The extension created a large, north-facing courtyard, which we paved. It's a large area that's perfect for the kids to ride their bikes and also for entertaining." This area has turned out to be a blessing and now houses a barbecue and table setting, which the family eat at most evenings. It's also handy to the vegie patch for those last-minute salad or herb additions.

The greenhouse/potting shed

Getting back to the organic essence of the garden, Jonathan says his potting shed is indispensable. "The potting shed has been great. I put that up myself, it's UV-proof plastic on a timber frame. You can go onto the internet and you can get plans for one. You can do anything these days with some quick-set cement and a few posts," says Jonathan.

The plastic-covered greenhouse/potting shed is where all the vegetable seedlings are raised. Says Jonathan: "I get a lot of seeds from catalogues, especially the heirloom varieties from

Digger's Seeds. They're great. I start all my seeds in the potting shed. Being in a cool climate area, being able to start things like tomatoes early in the season, when the frosts are still about, is a huge thing. I would highly recommend some type of greenhouse set-up even if it's only a small one on the ground with a few seed-raising trays covered with UV plastic. I raise my tomato seeds under cover, so they're protected from the frosts. With a greenhouse giving you that early start, you can get three crops in a summer."

The vegie patch

The vegetable patch, with its compost-rich soils, is a huge success. In the summer it produces hundreds of tomatoes and beans, loads of capsicums, chillies and eggplants and plenty of leafy greens. Says Jonathan: "I've learned to put in things that are eaten quickly, so we're erring on the side of leafy greens and things that can be eaten quickly because that's what the kids like, so there's not a lot of Brussels sprouts!"

In winter, the vegetable patch still yields a wealth of goodies including Maria's favourite, potatoes. Jonathan says: "I find winter is a much more productive time. The conditions are softer,

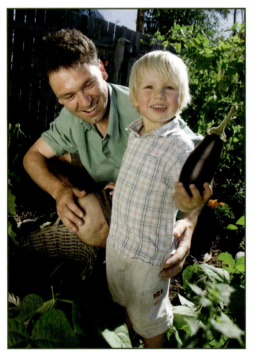

there are fewer pests and better conditions to work in. And all your Asian greens such as bok choy and choy sum come up so quickly. The whole vegie garden in winter can be just Chinese vegies plus broccoli and cabbage, the whole thing. They're quick and easy and we just eat so much of them. With all that iron and calcium, the leafy greens are the way to go."

Being organic (and pesticide-free) does present some challenges, but the results are absolutely worth it. Says Jonathan: The only things I put on the garden are Seasol and compost, that's it. I've never used any pesticides, herbicides ever," says Jonathan.

Companion planting

In a further effort to never use any pesticides or chemicals, Jonathan has included many companion plants in the vegie garden. "There are quite a lot of herbs in there, quite a lot of other plants there that act as companion plants," says Jonathan. "There are rows of marigolds with the lettuces. You brush by the marigolds and when you notice the pungent smell you think 'what is that'? If I was a nematode there's no way I'd want to be chewing on anything there. And rosemary puts them all off, too. Companion planting is huge."

Chook house

The chook house matches the other garden structures like the kids' cubby house and the tool shed which were erected at the same time. Jonathan made three entry points to the chook house:
- a normal-sized door for human access to the inside of the chook house.
- a smaller doorway, with a ramp to the chook's yard—purely for the chooks' use, but the kids favour this route too!
- a couple of flaps that open directly to the laying boxes, located outside the chook house, so the family can collect the eggs without having to enter the chook pen.

The chooks have a small, completely enclosed yard in which they are always safe to roam. Daily they are let out into the fenced pond and fruit tree area and specific parts of the vegie patch to clean things up, eat pests and fertilise as they go!

Jonathan and Maria have tried a couple of different chook breeds over the last three years and now have a clear favourite: "After having ISA Browns, White Leghorns and Black Australorps, definitely Black Australorps are the better breed," says Jonathan. "They're better with the kids, more approachable, there are less freak-outs and they seem to be more consistent with laying." They are also a very pretty, rotund style of chook!

Composting

The whole family appreciates the compost but Jonathan cherishes it. "I'm quite regimental in the kitchen about what goes where," he says. "There's a worm farm, a compost heap and chickens, so there are three places for kitchen scraps to go. Coffee grounds, potato skins, onion peels and chopped-up citrus are all no good for chickens, so they go in the compost, along with a few other things here and there, but pretty much everything else will go to the chickens and the worm farm.

"The compost is more industrial than just putting the kitchen scraps in the compost. I generate a lot of compost with a mix of lucerne and sheep manure, plus chicken manure. There are three layers: a layer of lucerne (one biscuit approx 7.5cm thick), a layer of either Dynamic Lifter or what's in the chicken coop, and some rotted sheep manure (plus the kitchen scraps that don't go to the chickens). Then I layer that again and multiply that by 10, wetting everything down. When you've got a metre cubed in volume the next day it will be 70 degrees inside the heap. I'm not kidding—you put a thermometer in there! I'm a scientist and it's what I do—I measure everything!

"Then in four weeks the whole thing will be ready to go straight onto the vegie garden. I fork it into the soil and then water it in and it's done. Adding compost puts all the right trace elements into the soil—the macro and micro nutrients. That's why the soil here is so viable, crumbly and black! In fact I love the soil more than I love the plants. Is that weird? It's bizarre!"

We think it's just fine to love the soil most of all. Really. It's OK.

Water tanks

Even though they live in a high-rainfall area, the family have ensured that all the water that falls on the roof is harvested into water tanks. All up they have five tanks and additional giant

overflow bins in which to store water. The two biggest 5000-litre tanks are plumbed to the vegie garden and some of the smaller tanks irrigate the many little pots of herbs and flowers around the house, as well as other parts of the garden.

Aquaponics

Jonathan uses the pond for another organic project, aquaponics. He explains: "Aquaponics is an experiment, and being a science teacher I like to experiment."

The system works on a simple principle of water circulation that uses nutrients from the pond water to grow herbs and vegetables and then returns the clean, filtered water to the pond. "You can have ebb or flow or continuous flow. I've got ebb and flow, which means I'm reticulating pond water that is rich in nitrogenous waste

from the fish, their wee and their poo," says Jonathan. "Water is pumped through the gravel bed and as it falls through there bacteria break down the nitrogen compounds into other nitrogen compounds that the plants can use as their source of food. The plants draw up those nitrogen compounds and grow—that's the hydroponics system of it—and then the filtered, clean water flows back into the pond.

The happy continuing story

Jonathan and Maria's efforts have really paid off. They're happy and the kids are happy. There is still some maintenance, but it's easy and enjoyable. Says Jonathan: "All the hard work has been done now to get the quality of the soil right. All I've got to do is put seeds in the greenhouse, they come up and then I transfer them into the vegie patch and that's it. There's drip irrigation on a timer and all I need to do is just a bit of weed control. Otherwise I don't have to touch the vegie patch. I just go back later and there's the crop! So that's the minimal energy input that you want, no big energy expenditure for maximum results."

Says Maria: "The best thing is having the kids grow up with it, being able to go out there and pick their own tomatoes. Isabella is trying out everything that's there. She's able to go outside and run around and harvest things, she helps to put seeds in and can see the whole process. Hopefully through that one day she'll really value the food. I'm very proud of what Jono has done. That's the one thing that I love most about this place, the garden we've got now. I love the house as well, but the garden is special."

What to grow

A-Z of vegetables

On the following pages we provide growing and care tips for all the backyard vegies, herbs and fruit you are likely to want to grow in your backyard. Please take time to read these tips, as they include advice on when is the best time to plant them, how to water and feed them, and which pests and diseases to look out for. See page 269 for our tips on growing herbs, and see page 247 for our tips on growing backyard fruit trees and vines.

Our ratings system

Some vegies are easier to grow than others, and pests and diseases can be more of a problem for certain plants, so we have devised a simple ratings system to give you an idea of how easy each vegetable is to grow at home.

 One pea means it's super-easy; great for beginners.

 Two peas is still easy, but these plants need a bit more care.

 Three peas means job satisfaction: grow these well and feel proud.

Artichoke

Ease of growing

Sowing time: plant in late autumn in mild-winter areas; late winter or early spring in cold-winter areas. Not suitable for the tropics or subtropics.

Growing tips: these are big thistles which grow at least a metre across. For the space they consume artichokes are not very productive so only grow them if you adore them or if you have a big garden. Artichokes do best where winters are rainy and cool but not sharply frosty. They like a mild summer so do well near the coast or in southern regions.

How to plant: suckers are a better choice than seed which can produce plants of variable quality. Plant suckers about 15cm deep and a metre apart and apply pelletised chicken manure around them. Water in and keep lightly moist

Routine care: the need for water increases as the plants grow and the weather warms up. Apply more chicken manure in spring and mulch around plants with rotted cow manure. In the first year, allow only the two strongest flower stems to grow—cut out all others as soon as they begin to emerge. In later years keep the four strongest stems only. Flower stems often branch, producing secondary flower buds. If you wish you can remove all or some of these to concentrate energy into the main bud. In autumn, cut plants to the ground and apply pelletised chicken manure and mulch. In the late autumn of the third year, dig up, divide and replant a young, strong division to reinvigorate and return the plant to its allotted space.

Ready to pick: cut when bud scales are still tight. Artichokes become stringy when the scales open out and are inedible once any part of the purple flower is seen. The first buds are ready in August or September and will continue to come until about November.

Watch for: aphids which cluster on developing flower buds; spray with soap spray such as Natrasoap.

In pots? Yes, But choose a deep container at least 60cm across.

Artichoke vegetables we eat are actually the unopened flower buds. Many gardeners grow an artichoke plant or two purely for their ornamental silvery leaves and big mauve-blue blooms.

Asian greens

Ease of growing

These are all related plants from the cabbage (brassica) family, including Chinese cabbage (wombok), Chinese broccoli (gai lan) and Chinese chard (bok choy, pak choy), tatsoi, choy sum, plus various others.

Sowing time: sow year-round in tropics and subtropics; July–May in temperate zones; Aug–Mar in cool zones.

Growing tips: all are compact, fast-growing leafy greens which like the same rich, well-drained, fertile soil plus plenty of sunshine and a steady supply of water. The faster you can grow them, the better they taste. All tend to do best in the cooler months, but if you try growing them in summer keep them well-watered.

How to plant: all grow easily from seed, but seedlings are readily available. Sow seed into a garden bed prepared in advance with plenty of compost and well-rotted animal manure dug in—see the seed packet for sowing depths and spacings for each vegetable.

Routine care: once seedlings are 15cm tall, liquid feed fortnightly to keep plants growing rapidly.

Ready to pick: it's best to harvest whole plants of Chinese cabbage and Chinese chard, rather than pick a few leaves, and you can harvest plants before they fully mature, if they're needed that night. However, with Chinese broccoli (gai lan), you can 'pick and come again', harvesting just as many stalks as you need—more will grow back.

Watch for: snails and slugs will eat seedlings, and caterpillars can be a pest, too (see page 280 for how to control these). Plants grow almost too fast sometimes, so it's best to get into sowing just a few seeds once a fortnight, to keep up a steady supply and avoid gluts.

In pots? Yes, but the bigger the pot the better the results, and regular watering is essential.

What to grow

Asian spices

Ease of growing

These include ginger (pictured above), galangal (top right), turmeric and lemon grass.

Best climate: all these plants thrive in warm climate zones, but you can grow them during summer in temperate and cool zones, too. Plant them any time of year in the tropics and subtropics; Sept–Dec in temperate zones; Oct–Dec in cool zones.

Growing tips: ginger, galangal and turmeric are all members of the ginger family and need similar growing conditions of moist, fertile soil enriched with compost and manure, plus plenty of warmth. Ginger and turmeric can cope with full sunshine, but galangal prefers part-shade. Lemon grass is a tropical grass which grows to form a clump and thrives in fertile, moist soil in full sunshine.

How to plant: plant shop-bought roots of ginger or turmeric 10–15cm deep, galangal 20cm deep, with shoots or buds pointing up, cover with soil and water well. Plant lemon grass seedlings, available from nurseries, into rich soil or pots, and water well. Lemon grass can also be grown from seed sown in spring in temperate zones, or at any time of year in the tropics and subtropics. Existing clumps of lemon grass can also be dug up, divided and replanted to start up several new clumps, if needed.

Routine care: keep up a steady supply of water and give all these plants monthly liquid feeds. In temperate and cool zones, all these plants might die back over winter (depending on how cool it gets), so if this happens cut back plants to ground level, feed with more manure, and they should re-shoot in spring. If they don't die back you don't need to do anything, but if they do look tatty in winter, tidy them up as much as you need to and give them a feed of manure in early spring.

Ready to pick: for ginger, galangal and turmeric, harvest in autumn, when the plants begin to die down (in temperate and cool zones) but in the tropics harvest plant roots as needed, replanting any roots which are not needed in the kitchen. With lemon grass, cut off stalks at the base, as needed in the kitchen.

Watch for: relatively trouble-free, the main thing these plants need is constant moisture. Snails will hide out in clumps, but they don't do a lot of damage. If these plants like their growing conditions, they can spread fairly rapidly, so in warm zones you may need to dig up clumps to control their size.

In pots? Yes, all of these plants grow well in pots, but they need very regular watering to thrive.

Asparagus

Ease of growing

Sowing time: plant crowns in winter. Not suitable for the tropics, or subtropics; poor in areas where winters are mild.

Growing tips: asparagus are long-lived perennials but are not highly productive for the space they need. They need a cold winter and, given that, a well-prepared bed will remain productive for many years. Dig the planting site deeply and enrich with plenty of compost or rotted manure. Except in areas where the soil is naturally alkaline, work in a handful of dolomite lime for each metre of bed. Loose, light soils are better than dense, clay soils.

How to plant: plant two-year old crowns in a 25cm-deep trench dug into the prepared ground. Make low mounds in the trench 40cm apart in rows 80cm apart. Place one crown on each, spreading the roots out evenly. Cover with 5cm of soil. When the spears begin to grow above the soil, add another 5cm of soil. Continue until the trench is refilled.

Routine care: keep evenly and deeply moist whenever the plant is in growth. In autumn the plants begin to die back for the winter. When all the ferny tops are dead, cut them off at ground level, and spread organic fertiliser around the plants. Water in well and mulch with a 3cm-deep layer of rotted cow manure.

Ready to pick: asparagus are the young shoots which emerge from the ground. Don't cut any spears in the first spring after planting. In the second spring, cut spears for one month from the time they first

Asparagus plants are either male or female. Males produce the best spears and asparagus crowns are always males only. If you grow the plants from seed, dig up and discard any which develop red berries in their second autumn, as they are females.

emerge. In subsequent years you can cut spears for three months. You must allow later spears to develop into leafy tops, or the plants decline. Cut spears when 15–20cm tall. Use a sharp knife and cut just below the surface of the soil.

Watch for: weak, spindly growth which is usually the result of insufficient nutrition. Asparagus is a heavy feeder so increase the dose of fertiliser given in late autumn. The plant is largely unaffected by pests.

In pots? Not suitable.

Beans

Ease of growing

Sowing time: sow seed Oct–Jan, or anytime but the wet season in the subtropics and tropics.

Growing tips: easiest and cheapest to start from seed, beans are warm season vegies that grow as either 2m-tall twining climbers or low, free-standing bushes. The climbers give the most beans but must be grown up a supporting stake or on wire mesh. The bush types are less productive but need little or no support and crop a bit sooner.

How to plant: push seed into pre-moistened soil to the depth of the second joint on your first finger. Cover with soil but don't water-in until the next day. Water sparingly until seedlings emerge in a week.

Routine care: as plants grow, water often enough to keep the soil moist, just below the surface. Once a month feed with liquid fertiliser. Train twining stems onto a supporting trellis or stake and, when the vine reaches the top, pinch out the growing tip with your fingers.

Ready to pick: pick beans when about 15cm long and before you can see the beans swelling inside the pod. Snip rather than pull the beans from the plant to avoid damaging the remaining stems.

Watch for: edges of leaves will go brown and curl if weather is very hot and/or windy. Plants usually recover with milder conditions. Whiteflies are tiny flying insects which cluster on the undersides of leaves. They fly up in a cloud when disturbed but quickly resettle. The insects suck sap and cause a fine mottling on the leaves. They also spread plant diseases. Hang sticky yellow traps to lure them away.

In pots? Yes, if you grow the smaller bush beans.

Broad beans

Ease of growing

Sowing time: sow Apr–Jun in the tropics and subtropics; Apr–Jul in mild-winter areas; Mar–Apr and Jul–Aug in cold-winter areas.

Growing tips: plants aren't climbers but they do become top heavy so some support is needed. Alternatively, choose dwarf varieties which grow to about 60cm tall (rather than 1m or more for taller types).

How to plant: a few weeks before sowing sprinkle a handful of dolomite lime along each metre of planting row and dig it in. At planting time, water the soil well the night before. The next day, push the big seeds into the moist ground to the depth of your second finger joint. Don't water again until the soil starts to go dry. Help plants support each other by sowing in double rows where plants and rows are spaced 20cm apart. Leave about 90cm between each double row for access.

Routine care: keep lightly, evenly moist—never sodden and never dry for days. Apply organic fertiliser either side of the plants when they emerge and again when about 30cm tall.

Ready to pick: if picking when pods are small, slice and cook like regular green beans. As beans grow, the outer pod becomes too tough to eat, but shell and eat the beans inside for a delicious treat. Pick often to maximise pod production.

Watch for: in drizzly or humid weather, the plants may be affected by powdery mildew. At first sign of powdery white spots on leaves spray daily with milk spray.

In pots? No; the small crop you'd get is not worth the effort.

Broccoli

Ease of growing

Sowing time: sow seeds Mar–May in the tropics and subtropics, Jan–May in mild-winter areas, Nov–Mar in cold-winter areas. Alternatively, plant seedlings during the same periods, plus one month.

Growing tips: broccoli varieties take 2–4 months to reach maturity during the cooler months. In very cold areas aim for maturity either before or after the coldest months of the year. Broccoli is easy to grow as long as you have pre-prepared the soil with rotted manure and low-nitrogen fertiliser.

How to plant: sow seeds directly into well dug-over soil that has been broken down to a fine texture. Make shallow trenches 45cm apart and sow seeds along them, also 45cm apart. Cover, moisten and expect germination in a week to 10 days. Don't plant too many. We recommend four to five plants every two to three weeks of the sowing period.

Routine care: keep plants moist at all times and water over monthly with liquid organic fertiliser. Check plants daily, especially under the leaves, for caterpillars and remove any weeds as they appear.

Ready to pick: cut the central head as soon as it is a useful size. Doing so encourages more side heads to develop. Broccoli is the unopened flower head and if you see yellow blooms, you have left it too late.

Watch for: caterpillars of the white butterfly. When you see butterflies flitting near broccoli, look under leaves for their tiny yellow eggs. Rub off at once. Spray with Dipel or Success to control actual caterpillars. Use soap spray to control aphids.

In pots? Plants are too big so crop yield from a pot is small, but if you want to give it ago, it should work, but you'll get just a few heads.

> **There are** several different varieties of broccoli which vary in the length of time they take to mature. Sowing four to five of each at the same time will result in a longer cropping season. As the early-maturing types finish, the mid-season varieties will take over, followed by the late-season broccoli.

Sprouts take from 14–20 weeks to start cropping, but you can have two crops by sowing your first batch of seeds at the start of the sowing period and another batch of seeds four to six weeks later.

Brussels sprouts

Ease of growing

Sowing time: sow seeds Dec-Mar in mild-winter areas, Oct-Feb in cold-winter areas. Alternatively, plant nursery-bought seedlings during the same periods, plus one month more. Not suitable for the tropics and sub-tropics.

Growing tips: Brussels sprouts are really only well suited to areas with quite cold winters so, in mild-winter areas, we'd only recommend them to those who love this vegetable. Where autumns and winters are mild, the sprouts often develop loosely, not tightly firm. At planting time, position a bamboo stake next to each seedling and tie in the stem as it grows to stop it from blowing over.

How to plant: sow seeds thinly into pots or seedling trays. Keep moist and lightly shaded until germination then move into full sun. They are ready to transplant into their growing positions about two months after germinating. Transplant into soil that was enriched for a previous crop as sprouts do not perform well in recently heavily-manured soil. They are not as successful in sandy soils as they are in clay based-soils.

Routine care: sprouts are shallow-rooted and keeping them moist is a regular and fairly frequent job. As they grow, water over every month or so with a liquid organic fertiliser and, when sprouts are starting to form, run a band of pelletised chicken manure along the plants.

Ready to pick: the lowest sprouts are ready to pick first and they should be harvested at golf-ball size. Cropping continues for several weeks.

Watch for: caterpillars of the white butterfly. When you see butterflies, spray plants with Dipel or Success and repeat weekly from then on. Use soap spray to control aphids.

In pots? Yes. Use a wide pot for maximum number of plants which are spaced 50cm apart. Grow in full sun in a sheltered spot to prevent wind damage.

Carrots

Ease of growing

Sowing time: Feb-Nov in tropics and subtropics; Jul–Mar in temperate zones; Sept–Feb in cool zones.
Growing tips: carrots like rich, well-drained, loose, crumbly soil that is not over-fertilised, and full sunshine.
How to plant: sowing from seed is preferable, but seedlings are readily available. Prepare soil thoroughly, down to a depth of 30cm, and get rid of all rocks, stones, old roots etc so the soil is fine and crumbly. Sow seed 6mm deep in rows 20–30cm apart. As seed is fine, you'll probably need to thin seedlings out to 3cm apart after they sprout—do this when seedlings are 5cm tall. Do a second thinning when seedlings are 15cm tall, so plants are 5cm apart.
Routine care: liquid feed fortnightly with a complete, balanced fertiliser once the seedlings are 15cm high, but do not overfeed, and avoid high-nitrogen fertilisers. Keep up a steady supply of water, and don't let the soil become dry.
Ready to pick: see the seed packet, but most carrots are ready to harvest 12–16 weeks after sowing seed.
Watch for: carrots will become mis-shapen if the roots hit stones, rocks etc in the soil, if the plants are over-crowded, or if the soil is over-fertilised with manure. Over-feeding causes more problems than under-feeding, so go easy on the fertiliser.
In pots? Yes, but make sure pots are deep enough for the roots to grow. Try 'Early Chantenay' or 'Baby' for growing carrots in pots.

Cauliflower

Ease of growing

Sowing time: sow seed Feb–Mar in mild-winter areas, Jan–Feb in cold-winter areas. Alternatively, plant bought seedlings Mar–Apr in mild-winter areas, Feb–Mar in cold-winter areas. Not suitable for the tropics and subtropics.

Though white is the colour we expect in cauliflower, there are varieties with green or purple curds and also hybrids between broccoli and cauliflower.

Growing tips: cauliflowers come in many varieties including 'minis', which are smaller plants with smaller heads. More importantly, different varieties take a longer or shorter time to mature. The quickest take about 10 weeks, the slowest 20–26 weeks and there are intermediate varieties between the two. By planting some of each you can crop over a long period. Cauliflower seedlings need warm weather to grow to production-size but don't like hot weather when the curds (the edible parts) are developing.

How to plant: sow seeds of mini cauliflowers into fine soil, directly where they are to grow. Sow seeds of standard-sized caulis into small pots or seedling trays and transplant into the garden bed when 7cm tall. Buying seedlings from the nursery cuts out that process but be careful to choose only relatively small seedlings with strong stems. Dig in dolomite lime (a handful per square metre) and manure or organic fertiliser a few weeks prior to planting. Always space cauliflower seedlings at the spacing stated on the packet—they don't take to crowding.

Routine care: keep lightly, evenly moist. Feed plants fortnightly with liquid, organic fertiliser or sprinkle a small handful of pelletised chicken manure around each plant monthly. When you first see a curd developing in the middle of the plant, crack and fold an outer leaf or two over the curd to prevent yellowing, frost damage and water spotting. Tie them into place.

Ready to pick: pick when curds are full-sized but still tightly packed. Quality deteriorates fast when curds begin to open up.

Watch for: caterpillars attack plants from the moment you plant them. Spray with non-toxic Dipel or Success each week or frequently check for caterpillars and squash by hand. Aphids are also attracted to cauliflowers—treat with soap spray.

In pots? Yes, but only mini cauliflowers are suitable and you'll need a big box as plants are spaced 30cm apart.

What to grow

Chillies & capsicums

Ease of growing

Sowing time: year-round in tropics and subtropics; Sep–Dec in temperate zones; Oct–Nov in cool zones.

Growing tips: these plants need warm weather, plus full sunshine and well-drained soil. Frosts will kill them, so delay sowing until all danger of frost has passed.

How to plant: they grow equally well from seed or seedlings. If raising from seed, sow seed in punnets kept in a warm spot, and plant out seedlings when they are 15cm tall. Plant sizes vary from 25cm tall to over 1m, so follow the seed packet or seedling label directions for correct spacings for plants. Prepare soil as for any vegetables prior to planting. In cooler zones, delay sowing or planting until overnight temperatures are mild, with days warm to hot.

Routine care: liquid feed young, growing plants fortnightly with a balanced fertiliser, then when plants start to flower and set fruit, change to a side-dressing of a complete fertiliser applied to the soil once a month. Keep plants evenly watered especially in warm, dry weather.

Ready to pick: pick fruit as needed. Let capsicums grow to the size you see in the shops, then harvest. Capsicums ripen from green to red. They are most sweet when fully ripe. Chillies can be harvested when you need them. They will change colour over time, so just harvest them as you need them whether they be green, yellow, orange or red.

Watch for: larger capsicum plants can be affected by strong winds, so add a stake to support plants. Seedlings can be attacked by caterpillars and snails, but they're usually trouble-free once established. In cool zones frost is a major problem. In hot weather in all areas, keep up the water supply to them

In pots? Yes, chillies grow easily in pots. Capsicum plants need a large, around 40cm in pot diameter.

Corn

Ease of growing

Sowing time: sow seeds Mar–Aug in tropics, Jul–Oct in subtropics, Sep–Jan in mild-winter areas, Oct–Dec in cold-winter areas.

Growing tips: corn takes up a fair bit of space but it's still a great tasting vegie to grow. As the cobs do not keep in good condition for long, plant a small batch every three weeks. Always position tall-growing corn on the south side of the vegie patch so it doesn't shade smaller crops.

How to plant: into soil that has recently been enriched with rotted manure, sow two seeds together every 30cm in blocks of at least two rows spaced 50cm apart. Don't sow in one long row as corn is wind pollinated and needs to be grown in a block. When seedlings emerge, remove the smaller of the two seedlings at each sowing spot. Water in and water just enough to keep the soil lightly moist until germination is complete.

Routine care: gradually increase watering as plants grow and weather warms. Daily or twice daily watering is needed in hot weather. Scatter pelletised chicken manure around growing plants monthly.

Ready to pick: when the silks die off and turn brown, cobs are generally ready to pick. Harvest by snapping off and aim to cook the cobs immediately after picking. You'll get one to three cobs per plant.

Watch for: grubs can bore into cobs. Prevent with weekly applications of Dipel or Success. Aphids almost always congregate under the outer leaves protecting the cobs, but these are mostly harmless.

In pots? No—plants are too tall and have too great a water need.

> The **Supersweet corn** varieties have the best taste that kids will love. When male flowers appear at the top of plants, shaking the plants in still weather distributes the pollen onto the female silks below. When it's close to harvest time, test by removing the leafy sheaths to expose corn kernels. If a milky fluid oozes out when a thumbnail is pushed into a kernel, the cob is perfect.

Cucumber

Ease of growing

Sowing time: sow seeds all year in the tropics, Sep–Mar in the subtropics, Oct–Jan in mild-winter areas, Oct–Dec in cold-winter areas.

Growing tips: cucumbers grow easily from seed sown where it is to grow but the seeds are highly sensitive to cold soil so don't be in too much of a rush to sow them in early spring. You may also find that fruit doesn't set in December and January and that's because plants tend to produce only male flowers when days are longest. Cucumbers like soil that's rich in rotted organic matter and neutral or barely acid (pH 6.5-7). To save space, sow cucumber seeds against a sunny fence and allow the vines to climb up a length of wire mesh. Alternatively, there are bush varieties which don't run everywhere.

How to plant: sow the big seeds where they are to grow by just pushing below the surface. Soil temperature has to be at least 15°C or the seeds may rot and the warmer the soil the faster they'll come up.

Routine care: keeping the plants evenly moist is the main regular task with cucumbers. As long as the soil was well manured prior to planting a monthly watering with a liquid organic fertiliser is all the additional feeding needed. If you let cucumbers run across the ground, pinching out the growing tips of stems will stop the spread—but only do that once fruit has set on those stems.

Ready to pick: pick small and pick often. If you let cucumbers grow too big and old they can become bitter and tough. When they're the size you are familiar with, that's when to pick. If you want them for gherkins, pick very small.

Watch for: mildew commonly affects cucumber leaves. Have milk spray handy and spray on leaves every second day as a preventative measure. It is less effective once mildew is present.

In pots? Yes, select bush types or place the pot against a length of trellis attached to a fence.

> **For easiest growth,** look for disease-resistant varieties and also day-length-neutral types. Some are marketed as 'burpless' and you should plant these if belching is a problem for you after eating cucumbers.

There are hundreds of types of eggplants in all sorts of shapes, sizes and colours and with a variety of tastes. You'll only find unusual varieties in the catalogues of specialist seed suppliers.

Eggplant

Ease of growing

Sowing time: sow seeds Sep–Mar in tropical and subtropical areas, Sep–Dec in mild-winter areas, Oct–Nov in cold-winter areas. Alternatively, plant seedlings in these periods.

Growing tips: related to tomatoes, but even more-cold sensitive, eggplants are only successful in the warmest months. In areas where summer nights can be cool, you may only be able to fruit them with the help of the heat radiated by a sunny masonry wall or in pots sat on a concrete drive. There are two main types—the traditional, tear-drop shaped fruit and the eggplant which is more the shape and size of a zucchini. Apart from all-day sun and shelter from wind, eggplants have no special needs. Plants grow 80cm tall and you'll get perhaps seven fruit per plant.

How to plant: sow two or three seeds in each 10cm pot to ensure success. On germination, select the best looking seedlings and snip off the others at the base. Keep moist, place in sheltered full sun and feed fortnightly with liquid fertiliser. Plant out at 60cm spacings when seedlings are 15cm tall. Alternatively, plant seedlings directly into the vegie patch in warm weather.

Routine care: keep very lightly moist when plants are young but increase frequency and volume of water when fruits begin to develop. If more than seven fruits set, remove the extras so that those remaining grow properly. Water monthly with liquid organic fertiliser. You may need to support plants with a slim bamboo stake.

Ready to pick: pick when fully coloured and before the skin starts to wrinkle. Eggplants will turn bitter if left on the plant too long.

Watch for: caterpillars which chew holes into leaves and bore into fruit—control with Dipel or Success applied weekly. Mites multiply on the undersides of leaves in hot, dry weather. They're hard to control but try PestOil.

In pots? Yes; grow one plant per 40cm pot.

Garlic

Ease of growing

Growing time: Mar–Jul in tropics and subtropics; Apr–Aug in temperate zones; Mar–Sept in cool zones.
Growing tips: garlic is best suited to areas with cool, frosty winters. In warmer areas, choose 'softneck' varieties suited to warm climates. Garlic generally likes full sun and light, well-drained soil.
How to plant: add compost or well-rotted manure to the bed before planting, then plant cloves 5cm deep, with the pointed end facing upwards, spaced 15–20cm apart. In warmer climates, refrigerate cloves for a week before planting, water in with chilled water after planting.
Routine care: liquid-feed monthly after the first shoots appear, or scatter around pelletised chicken manure while plants are growing. Increase watering of plants, especially during hot weather.
Ready to pick: dig up bulbs when leaves have turned yellow and are starting to die off; hang up the plants to dry in a dry, airy spot.
Watch for: garlic isn't subject to many pests once growing well (but snails and slugs can eat new shoots). Well-drained soil is essential to prevent fungal diseases developing, especially in wet weather. In warm zones your crop simply may fail, due to the lack of midwinter chilling, which it needs to set cloves. Choose a variety suited to your climate zone.
In pots? Not really, but you can try if you like. Pots need to be kept cool on warm days, to keep soil temperatures downs, so place your pot of garlic inside another, larger pot, to help keep it cool.

Grapes

Ease of growing

Best climate: grapes are not suited to the humid tropics and subtropics, but they can be grown in temperate and cool climate zones, They do best in areas of low humidity, so they're not ideal for areas such as the NSW coast. For backyards, choose table grape varieties, not wine grapes.

Growing tips: grapevines need well-drained soil and full sunshine, plus a frame to climb upon (eg, a pergola or trellis).

How to plant: grapes are deciduous vines, so it's best to plant them while dormant in winter as bare-rooted plants. To plant, dig a planting hole, create a conical mound of soil in the base of the hole then drape the bare roots over the mound, making sure that the swollen graft point that's low on the stem is above ground level. Back-fill with soil and water in.

Routine care: grapes need no fertilising if grown in fertile soil, but if grown in light, sandy soils, give them a once-a-year feed with Dynamic Lifter or citrus food in spring. Your main job in the first year will be tying rapidly growing canes to the climbing frame. In subsequent years, you'll need to prune back the framework of canes during winter, to promote the growth of new wood, on which fruit will be borne. For starters, just cut back the plant to keep the vine tidy. Another good job each year is to thin out the number of bunches of grapes forming, to encourage the remaining bunches to grow to a good size and quality.

Ready to pick: grapes ripen in summer, so when bunches look like they are getting close to ripeness, taste-test a grape or two.

Watch for: in humid zones vines can be affected badly by fungal diseases. Sprays are available, including organic sprays, but also do what you can to increase air-circulation around your vine. Birds eating the fruit are another common problem.

In pots? No.

Leeks

Ease of growing

Sowing time: sow seeds Jan–Mar in tropical and subtropical areas, Dec–Mar in mild-winter areas, Oct–Mar in cold-winter areas. Alternatively, plant nursery-bought seedlings in those periods plus one month more.

Growing tips: raising them from seed is the best and cheapest method. They take anything from three to nearly six months to reach maturity from the time you transplant them (depending on the variety) and the slower-maturing types are generally the best. However, it can be a good idea to start both early and late-maturing leeks so you have a longer harvest period. Leeks need good, heavily enriched, neutral pH soil and small but frequent doses of organic fertiliser as they grow.

How to plant: sow seeds into pots or seedling trays. Sow thinly to avoid overcrowding and let seedlings grow on until about 20cm tall. Transplant seedlings by dropping into individual, narrow holes 15cm deep and watering in (make the holes with a slim, straight stick).

Routine care: keep lightly moist and growing with monthly feeds with a liquid organic fertiliser. Alternatively, run a band of pelletised chicken manure either side of plants once a month. If white stems are wanted, soil can be piled up around plants as they grow or you can build up a clean mulch of straw around them. Some gardeners slip a one-litre milk carton over plants to whiten the stems.

Ready to pick: pull leeks when the stems are 2–3cm thick. If they are not easily removed, dig them out to avoid breaking the stems.

Watch for: leeks are not much bothered by pests and diseases.

In pots? Yes; you won't get a big crop but styrofoam fruit boxes are a good shape and size for growing leeks.

Lettuce

Ease of growing

Sowing time: sow year-round in all areas (but seeds and seedlings don't do well in our hot summer weather).

Growing tips: lettuce needs full sunshine, rich, well-drained soil and a steady supply of water and fertiliser.

How to plant: lettuce grows easily from seed or seedlings. If raising from seed, either sow seed in punnets and plant out seedlings when 15cm tall, or sow seed directly where they are to grow in rows 20cm apart for smaller lettuce types, or 30cm part for larger ones (check the seed packet or seedling label and follow those guides for spacings). Lettuce loves steady moisture, so once seedlings are growing well, mulch the soil around plants.

Routine care: never let the soil dry out, and in summer give plants daily waterings if it doesn't rain. Liquid-feed fortnightly with a nitrogen-rich fertiliser to encourage leafy growth.

Ready to pick: start harvesting

leaves of loose-leaf lettuce (eg, Oakleaf) as soon as they are edible size, about four weeks after planting (pick the outer leaves first). 'Heart-forming' lettuce (such as 'Iceberg' and 'Cos') can be harvested when at the size you see in the shops.

Watch for: lettuce seed may fail to germinate in very hot weather, and seedlings can also 'bolt' (ie, grow too rapidly, going to seed fast) in very hot weather. Snails and slugs often eat seedlings, so watch for them.

In pots? Yes, an excellent choice for pots, but they need careful, regular watering and feeding in pots.

Melons

Ease of growing

Sowing time: sow seeds all year round in the tropics, Aug–Feb in the subtropics, Sep–Dec in mild-winter areas, Oct–Nov in cold-winter areas.

Growing tips: rockmelons, watermelons and honeydew melons take up a lot of space by sprawling across the ground and each plant only produces one to a few melons. Melons need a long, warm to hot growing season to ripen and can't be sown until the soil has warmed up well in spring. A big range of melons is available.

How to plant: sow seeds directly where they are to grow, allowing 1.5m between seedlings. Melons can be tricky to transplant as the roots break easily so direct sowing gives the best results.

Routine care: keep moist but don't overwater. As long as your soil is deep and moisture-retentive, melons don't need heavy watering but shouldn't be allowed to go dry when young and producing flowers. Once the fruit is approaching ripeness, reduce watering to concentrate sugars and flavour in the fruit. During the growing season, apply liquid organic fertiliser two to three times only. You can limit the spread of melons by pinching out the growing tip of a stem once it has set at least one melon.

Ready to pick: all melons change colour when nearing ripeness and rockmelons will often just disconnect from the vine when ripe. They also have a beautiful, ripe aroma. Watermelons develop a yellow patch where they touched the ground and the stem withers when ripe.

Watch for: melons suffer from mildew. Use a milk spray applied daily as a preventative measure.

In pots? No, the plants are too big.

It's not a staple crop but if you are familiar with okra and know how to use it, it's an easy plant to grow that produces well.

Okra

Ease of growing

Sowing time: sow seeds all year in the tropics, Aug–Feb in the subtropics, Sep–Dec in mild-winter areas, Oct–Nov in cold-winter areas.

Growing tips: okra is a hibiscus-relative which produces long, pointy seed pods after the flowers have fallen. It grows as a warm-season annual to about 1m tall and needs a long, hot growing season. The seed pods are the edible part. They are used in soups and stews, becoming gelatinous when cooked.

How to plant: sow seeds directly where they are to grow, allowing about 70cm between each sowing station. Always wait until moderately hot weather has arrived or the seeds may not germinate.

Routine care: grow okra quickly by keeping it evenly moist and fed once a month with liquid organic fertiliser. When flowering starts, add a monthly scattering of pelletised chicken manure.

Ready to pick: pods form straight after flowers fall and are ready to pick within a week when 5–8cm long. It's important to pick the pods whether you want them or not, as they will soon become too big and tough to eat if left on the bush to grow longer than 10cm and leaving them attached will also end flowering so no more pods will come.

Watch for: okra is not bothered by pests and diseases.

In pots? Yes, but plants are naturally rangy so don't think of them as an ornamental.

Onions
Ease of growing

Sowing time: sow seed in autumn in the tropics and subtropics, Mar–Jul in mild-winter areas, Apr–Sep in cold-winter areas. You can also plant seedlings in the same periods.

Growing tips: different onions take different lengths of time to mature and they're referred to as 'early' (quick to mature) 'mid-season' or 'intermediate' (medium time to mature) and 'late' (long time to mature). The longer they take the better they keep but late-maturing onions can take 30 weeks to grow full-size. Sow early varieties in autumn, mid-season types in winter and late varieties in late winter or early spring. Onions don't need excessively rich soil or high levels of manure.

How to plant: sow seeds into shallow trenches made in fine-textured soil directly where they are to grow. Cover and moisten with a fine mist. It's essential to keep them moist until germination, which may be four to five days or up to two weeks if the weather is cool. When seedlings emerge, thin out so the remainder are spaced 8cm apart. Bought seedlings are simply laid with their roots in a shallow trench at 8cm intervals. Once covered and watered in they will stand up over the following days.

Routine care: don't let weeds establish. Onions like regular rain or water but they're not as susceptible to drying out as are many leafy vegies. When the plants have grown reasonably large, mulch around them thinly with lucerne hay.

Ready to pick: pull when small for use as pickling or spring onions. However, they are fully mature when the leafy tops yellow off and fall over.

Watch for: mildews and rots. Minimise the chances of infection by growing only in all-day sun, being careful not to overwater and never using animal manures or compost at planting time or as a mulch.

In pots? No, it's not worth the effort for the crop you'll get.

As onions approach maturity, lengthen the time between waterings and finally let them go dry. Once pulled from the soil, lay them out in airy, broken shade for a week or two to dry out fully. Twist and pull the dead leaves to remove.

Other salad greens

Ease of growing

These include fast-growing rocket, mizuna and mustard.

Growing time: sow seed Mar-Jul in the tropics and subtropics; Mar-Nov in temperate and cool zones.

Growing tips: these fast-growing plants like well-drained soil and regular liquid feeds. They do well anywhere from full sun to partial sun, and grow better from seed, than seedlings. As they grow fast and become peppery when leaves become big, it's best to grow small crops, each two to three weeks apart, to keep up a steady supply.

How to plant: scatter seed lightly over smoothly raked soil and lightly cover with seed-raising mix or soil, and water in well. Germination is fast (less than a week) and growth is rapid. Thin out rocket seedlings to 10cm apart when 10cm tall; thin out mizuna and mustard seedlings to 20cm apart when 15cm tall.

Routine care: feed plants fortnightly with a half-strength liquid fertiliser, and they also need regular watering (daily in hot weather) to maintain rapid growth.

Ready to pick: harvest leaves when small, for a milder taste. As plants grow in size, their taste becomes hotter. When plants become too big and peppery, toss them on your compost heap and resow the next crop.

Watch for: snails and slugs can eat small seedlings, but generally these are pest-free. In hot weather they will tend to 'bolt' to seed rapidly.

In pots? Yes, they are well suited to pots but water well at all times.

Parsnips

Ease of growing

Sowing time: sow seeds Mar–May in mild-winter areas, Oct–Mar in cold-winter areas, not suitable for the tropics and subtropics.

Growing tips: this root vegetable takes five to six months to reach harvest size. The roots grow most sweet and delicious when the weather is very cold and it should always be sown to mature in the cooler months of the year. Seed should also be sown during cooler periods to maximise germination. Soil for parsnips must be loose, friable and free of rocks to a depth of at least 30cm as the roots will deform or fork if they encounter hardness.

How to plant: sow seeds directly where they are to grow and thin seedlings to 10cm apart. Keep lightly moist but don't expect to see seedlings for at least three weeks.

Routine care: don't let the plants go dry and nor should you allow weeds to establish near them. Parsnips are happy to grow in soil that has been enriched for a previous summer crop without additional manure or fertiliser being added

Ready to pick: you can pull baby parsnips anytime after three months after germination. They will take another three months to grow to full-size. Once full-sized, parsnips can remain in the ground for several months more without deterioration so you can pull them as you need them. If they are left in the ground over winter they will develop their sweetest and best flavour.

Watch for: mildew sometimes strikes parsnip foliage in humid or rainy weather. Treat with milk spray at first sign of mildew.

In pots? Yes, but in deep containers with a wide surface area.

Peas

Ease of growing

These include podded peas, snow peas and sugar snap peas.

Sowing time: sow Mar–July in tropics and subtropics; Feb–Jul in temperate zones; Jun–Sept in cool zones.

Growing tips: peas like fertile, well-drained, alkaline soil, plus full-sun (although some shade is OK). Most peas (except the dwarf types) are climbers and will need a trellis or wire frame about 1.5m high or more to grow on (eg, wire mesh attached to a fence). You can grow peas from seed or seedlings, but seed are cheapest and our preferred option.

How to plant: dig a few handfuls of lime into the soil when preparing the soil as for other vegies. Water the soil prior to planting, then sow seed 5cm deep, about 3–5cm apart. If sowing rows of peas, keep them 40–50cm apart. If the soil is already moist when planting, don't water in seed, and don't water until seedlings have emerged, unless the weather is sunny and dry. In that case water sparingly so soil is lightly moist.

Routine care: no extra fertilising is needed if you fertilised prior to planting, but mulch around plants to preserve soil moisture. To discourage weeds and support plants, build up a 'hill' of soil around the base of each plant.

Ready to pick: see the seed packet, but nine to 12 weeks after sowing seed you should get your first pods to harvest. Keep on harvesting pods as they appear, as this encourages more pods to form and will improve your yield from each plant.

Watch for: birds can sometimes eat emerging baby seedlings, so protect with netting, sticks, etc. Powdery mildew can be a problem with pea plants in humid areas (such as the East Coast) and you may lose your crop there in bad years. Watch for snails and slugs, but avoid weeding around the base of plants.

In pots? Dwarf peas can be grown in pots, but climbing types do better in larger troughs, with a trellis behind for the plants to climb on.

Potatoes

Ease of growing

Sowing time: plant seed potatoes Jan–Aug in tropics and subtropics; July–Oct and then Jan–Feb in temperate zones; Aug–Dec in cool zones.

Growing tips: buy certified 'disease-free' seed potatoes from nurseries and produce suppliers, to avoid the chance of disease and crop failure. Potatoes like well-drained, fertile, friable soil, and lots of sunshine, but they are very susceptible to frost. If your seed potatoes have more than one 'eye', you can cut them into separate decent-sized chunks, each of which will produce a whole plant. If you do cut up seed potatoes, let them dry out before planting.

How to plant: dig 15cm deep furrows 75cm apart, sprinkle complete fertiliser into the base of the furrow and cover with 5cm of soil. Then plant each seed potato with the eye facing up, spacing them 25–30cm apart. Cover with soil and water well. Sprouts should emerge in about three to four weeks.

Routine care: as they grow, start 'hilling' soil around the base of plants to protect them from wind and, later on, to prevent forming potato tubers being exposed to sunlight (which makes them green and, potentially, toxic). Regular watering is essential, but little extra fertilising is needed after planting.

Ready to pick: plants begin to form tubers after flowering finishes. At this stage the leaves start to yellow and die back. When leaves are fully yellow you can start harvesting 'new' potatoes, but if you wait a few weeks longer the potatoes will have grown bigger and more flavoursome. Instead of harvesting all your potatoes, just 'bandicoot' your way into a hill with your hands feeling for spuds, only pick just as many spuds as you need that night.

Watch for: various caterpillars can eat potato leaves, but unless the infestation is severe, don't worry about them. Extremely wet weather, such as happens in the tropics and subtropics, can ruin potato crops.

In pots? Yes, and in stacks of tyres, wire cages and anything else that holds straw, compost or soil. Using the 'no-soil' method of growing potatoes, all you need to do is plant tubers into compost and straw, then as plants grow keep on building up the straw and/or compost around the plants so you completely conceal all developing potato tubers.

Pumpkin

Ease of growing

Growing time: sow seeds Apr–Aug in the tropics; Aug–Dec and Feb–Mar in the subtropics; Sep–Dec in mild-winter areas; Oct–Dec in cold-winter areas.

Growing tips: fast-growing vines which can spread 2–3m or more, pumpkins demand a lot of space and, for standard-sized pumpkins, expect three to five fruit per plant. They love soil which contains plenty of rotted manure or other completely composted organic matter. Pumpkin plants produce separate male and female flowers which need bees to transfer pollen between them, or no pumpkins develop. In the absence of bees at flowering time, you can hand pollinate by collecting pollen from male flowers with a soft brush and dusting it into the female flowers. Female flowers are those with a tiny pumpkin at the point where the base of the flower joins its stem.

There is a huge range of pumpkins, many with flavours unlike those you may be used to. These are available from the catalogues of specialist seed suppliers.

How to plant: make a little mound of soil and push two or three seeds into it to guarantee at least one seedling comes up. When the seeds come up, pull out all but the biggest and best. Germination usually takes about a week but as seeds only germinate in warm conditions, if the soil or weather is too wet and cold they may not come up. You can buy pumpkins as seedlings but as the seeds are so easy to sow and germinate there's little point in the added expenditure.

Routine care: keep moist and don't allow competing weeds or grasses to establish in the area into which the pumpkins will spread. Two weeks after the seeds come up, water the soil but not the leaves with a fish or seaweed based liquid fertiliser and repeat the application each month thereafter. If stems start to grow much longer than you would like, cut off the growing tips to force side branches to develop.

Ready to pick: pumpkins take at least 14 weeks to mature and you can tell they're ready by the look of the stem which attaches the pumpkin to its vine. At maturity, it wrinkles and turns woody. The pumpkin itself may also have changed colour (depending on variety). Harvest by cutting from the vine leaving a short section of stem attached to the pumpkin. This acts as a cap to prevent rots from entering the fruit.

Watch for: pumpkins can be affected by powdery mildew, especially in wet, or hot and humid weather. Pumpkin beetle and leaf-eating ladybirds can munch on the leaves and leave the odd one skeletonised, but if the damage isn't severe, don't worry about it. And sometimes, rats and mice can dig up and eat the seeds and also gnaw on the fruit.

In pots? No. The vines are too big.

Radish

Ease of growing

Growing time: sow seeds all year in the tropics and subtropics; Aug–May in mild-winter areas; Sep–Apr in cold-winter areas.

Growing tips: radish are among the fastest of any vegetable to germinate and grow, so sow a short row each week and pull the crop constantly. They're easy to grow in average soil and you can sow them as an intercrop in the spaces between other vegies, pulling the radishes well before their presence interferes with the growth of the other vegies.

How to plant: sow seeds thinly in shallow trenches and barely cover. Water in and keep moist. Germination takes just a few days and is fastest in the warmer months.

Routine care: thin seedlings so each is spaced 2cm apart. Keep evenly moist but there's no need to feed if you planted them into fertile vegie patch soil. If you do feed, don't use a high-nitrogen soluble fertiliser. Don't let weeds establish and if nearby vegies start to shade them, remove the shade-casting leaves.

Ready to pick: pull your first radish a month after germination. If it is a satisfactory size, harvest at will. If too small, wait another week and try again. Radishes are best when young and small—they become too hot as they get bigger.

Watch for: nothing serious seems to afflict radishes.

In pots? Yes, an ideal potted vegie best suited to shallow pots.

Rhubarb

Ease of growing

Sowing time: plant 'crowns' (ie, two-year-old bare-rooted plants) Jul–Apr in the tropics and subtropics; July–Feb in temperate zones; Aug–Feb in cool zones. You can plant rhubarb seedlings at any time of year.

Growing tips: rhubarb does best anywhere from semi-shade to full sun in fertile, well-drained soil enriched with well-rotted manure and compost. Unlike most other vegies, rhubarb plants will keep on cropping for three or four years. At this stage, you can then lift, divide and replant the four-year-old clump in late winter or early spring to maintain good production. If you really want to have red rhubarb stems, it is best to grow plants from crowns of named varieties such as 'Sydney

---

Japanese or daikon radish produce long, white roots like big, smooth parsnips. They are sown in spring and autumn and can be harvested about 10 weeks after germination.

Crimson'. Rhubarb seedlings are often sold in nurseries, but be warned that the stem colour of these seedling-grown plants can be variable, and they may sometimes be green-stemmed. There is no major flavour difference between the red and green-stemmed varieties. It's mostly just a visual thing.

How to plant: prepare the bed as for other vegies, then plant crowns 75–90cm apart, with the top of the crowns just at or below the soil level.

Routine care: once new stalks emerge, liquid-feed every four to six weeks from spring through to autumn with a high-nitrogen fertiliser. During winter, when plants die down, fork in more compost and manure. Water plants regularly at all times, then after plants die back in winter, fork in more compost and rotted manure around plants.

Ready to pick: harvest when they're the same size as sold in the shops, but only pick the older, outer stalks from the base of the plant, and don't pick too many stalks from any one plant—just a few at the most each time. **Warning:** never eat rhubarb leaves, as they contain toxins.

Watch for: Snails and slugs can eat emerging baby stalks in spring.

In pots? Not suitable.

Shallots

Ease of growing

Also called spring onions, scallions, bunching onions, green onions

Sowing time: sow seed anytime but the wet season in the tropics and subtropics, anytime in mild-winter areas, anytime but winter in cold-winter areas. You can also plant nursery-bought seedlings in the same periods.

Growing tips: shallots are handy to have because you can pull them as you need them anytime after they're a size you consider usable. Those left in the ground just keep getting bigger, but only slowly. They demand no special growing treatment and don't seem to attract much in the way of pests and diseases. You can grow them in anything from all-day sun to about half a day's sun.

Instead of pulling shallots out of the ground, roots and all, try cutting them off just above ground level. They will often re-shoot, giving you a new plant for no effort whatsoever.

How to plant: sow seeds into shallow trenches directly where they are to grow. Aim for a spacing of 1cm to minimise the need for later thinning but sowing too many is not a problem as the plants can always be separated when harvesting. Cover and moisten with a fine mist. It's essential to keep the soil lightly moist but not sodden until germination, which takes about two weeks. Bought seedlings are separated into individuals and laid closely together with their roots in a shallow trench. Once covered and watered in they'll stand up over the following days.

Routine care: regular but not overly frequent watering is the main job. Once a month you can water them over with liquid organic fertiliser but, if the soil is good quality and fertile, that isn't really necessary.

Ready to pick: start to pull when you think they're big enough.

Watch for: shallots are largely trouble-free. Too much manure in the soil or used as mulch can encourage diseases and onion fly.

In pots? Yes, they're great in pots.

Silver beet

Ease of growing

Sowing time: sow year-round in tropics and subtropics; Jul–Mar in temperate zones; Aug–Feb in cool zones.

Growing tips: silver beet grows easily from seed or seedlings. All it needs is full sun and fertile, well-drained soil, plus a steady supply of moisture.

How to plant: sow silver beet seedlings 30cm apart, watering in well after planting. If growing from seed, sow seed 12mm deep in rows 30cm apart where they are to grow, water in well. Germination takes about 10–14 days.

Routine care: silver beet just needs a steady supply of water, plus liquid feeds with a nitrogen-rich plant food every fortnight.

Ready to pick: as soon as leaves become large enough to use in the kitchen, cut or twist off leaves low down on the stalk near the base of the plant, and new leaves will grow. If you have several plants, harvest just a few leaves from each to make up a bunch.

Watch for: snails and slugs will eat seedlings, and grasshoppers, katydids and caterpillars will munch holes in leaves. If the damage isn't too bad, don't worry about it.

In pots? Yes, but the larger the pot the better, and keep pots well watered at all times, liquid feeding fortnightly.

English spinach

Ease of growing

Sowing time: sow seeds May–Jun in the tropics and subtropics, Apr–Jul in mild-winter areas, Mar–Aug in cold-winter areas.

Growing tips: English spinach loves to grow during the cooler weather and quickly runs to seed when day temperatures start to become warm. However, if your winters are extremely cold with heavy frosts, time your sowing to avoid the worst frosts. Grow spinach in soil that has had manure or compost dug through it and which is reasonably moisture-retentive. Where winters are not very cold, spinach grows successfully in only half a day's sun.

How to plant: sow seeds in batches two to three weeks apart to ensure a continuous supply. Sow seed where it is to grow into moist soil 2–3cm deep and about 10cm apart. Later, pull out every second plant to allow the remainder to grow to full-size. Eat the thinnings as baby spinach. Some gardeners claim that soaking the seeds for a few hours before sowing improves germination.

Routine care: mulch around the young plants thinly with rotted manure or compost and be sure to water them regularly. The plants must not wilt at any time. Water them over fortnightly with liquid, organic fertiliser. Don't allow weeds to establish as these will compete for food and water.

Ready to pick: you can remove the outer leaves from individual plants about two months after they emerged as seedlings. Picked leaf by leaf, plants will crop for about a month, after which they should be pulled up.

Watch for: caterpillars and leaf miners which can be prevented with a weekly application of sprays of either Dipel or Success.

In pots? Yes, spinach grows well in pots and gives a worthwhile crop.

Originally from Central America, sweet potatoes are now in the top 10 of the world's most important food crops. Orange and white are the two most common types but there are varieties with purple, red and yellow flesh as well.

Sweet potato

Ease of growing

Growing time: plant tubers Jul–Mar in the tropics and subtropics; Sep–Nov in mild-winter areas. Not suitable for cold-winter areas.

Growing tips: sweet potatoes grow from the same tubers you eat (in much the same way as potatoes do). They are tropical, groundcovering vines which need a long, hot growing season to produce tubers. Each plant can spread 2m or more in all directions, which means they take up quite a lot of space for the crop they yield. The ideal soil for them is moisture-retentive yet fast-draining, open and loose rather than stiff and heavy, and it's not overly rich in manure or nitrogenous fertiliser.

How to plant: grow from bought tubers cut into big sections. Out of the tropics, put the tuber in a box, cover shallowly with moist sand and place in a warm spot. When shoots emerge, take out the tuber and cut into sections, each with a shoot. Plant these a metre apart, barely burying the tuber, into the top of a long, low mound of soil a metre wide at its base. In the tropics, you can do the same thing or just cut up the tuber, let it dry a day or two and plant as above. Tropical readers can also grow new plants from cuttings from an existing plant.

Routine care: keep the soil moist. The stems will root where they touch ground and more tubers will form there. However, the plants will spread indefinitely so it's a better idea to lift the stems off the ground every few days to stop them from rooting. When stems have reached the limit of their allotted space, snip off the growing tips. When you lift the stems, check for weeds and remove any that are growing.

Ready to pick: tubers will be ready to dig up after about 16 weeks in the tropics but more like 20 weeks in non-tropical, warm areas. Yellowing leaves are a sign of maturity. It's best to harvest all the tubers at once so if you have several plants, harvest only one, eat the crop then harvest another—they will keep in the ground. You can expect about eight tubers from each plant.

Watch for: not much attacks sweet potato in non-tropical areas but in the monsoonal tropics, sweet potato weevil is a pest of the leaves, stems and tubers. Avoid it by planting just one or two at a time and always harvesting all the tubers in one go. In the tropics, you could start a new batch once a fortnight.

In pots? Yes. You could grow one plant in a 45cm pot placed on a plinth so its stems could trail down.

Tomatoes

Ease of growing
Cherry tomatoes
Tall staking types

Sowing time: you can sow tomato seed year-round in the tropics and subtropics; Aug–Jan in temperate zones; Sept–Nov in cool zones.

Growing tips: tomatoes love warmth, rich, free-draining soil, a steady supply of water, and full sunshine, but they are frost-tender. Cherry tomatoes are relatively easy and trouble-free to grow, but the taller-growing types that need support from a stake and which produce larger fruit need more maintenance, especially in areas prone to fruit fly and other warm-climate pests and diseases.

How to plant: plant sizes vary widely, so see the seed packet or seedling label for the correct spacing and staking needs. If growing from seed, raise plants in a punnet in a warm spot and plant out seedlings when 15cm tall. If a plant is a tall-growing type which needs staking, add a tall tomato stake (2.4m tall) when planting the seedling. Prepare the soil in a sunny spot a few weeks before planting, but make sure to add a handful of lime for each planting spot, to help prevent the disease 'blossom end rot'. Thoroughly dig the lime through the soil.

Routine care: regular watering is vital for tomatoes, so never let the soil dry out. Apply a liquid plant food every fortnight after the plants start to develop flower buds. Inspect plants often for pests and other problems.

Staking tips: tie plants to stakes as they grow, to prevent damage from wind. Tall-growing tomatoes need support and the most common method is a tall stake. However, tomato plants branch freely which makes staking impossible. Experienced growers remove all side branches as they appear so plants grow as a single stem which is easy to tie to the stake at intervals. To do this, pinch out all laterals with your fingers as soon as they are seen. At planting time, examine the plant and remove any side branches which come from the main stem. Thereafter, new laterals will be produced in the leaf junction directly below each set of flowers. Rub these out as they appear. The result will be one tall stem with clusters of fruit all the way up.

Ready to pick: when the fruit start to change colour (usually from green to red) you can either bring them inside to ripen in a dark spot away from sunlight, or let the fruit ripen on the vine and hope you get to the fruit before any pests or birds do.

Watch for: caterpillars can eat leaves and snails can munch seedlings, but the main pest to watch for is fruit fly. If you live in a known fruit fly area, take control measures as a matter of course—don't wait until you see them. Organic controls such as Yates Nature's Way Fruit Fly Killer and Eco-Naturalure are available, but they need frequent applications to work well. Other, non-organic control options are available, so talk to your local garden centre about them. Derris Dust and Tomato Dust are low-toxicity powders to sprinkle on tomato plants to control both pests and diseases. With these, however, you'll have to wait a day or two until the tomatoes are safe to eat (see the product labels for details.) Generally, small cherry tomatoes are bothered much less by pests and diseases than the bigger plants. You can also help to avoid tomato plant diseases by not growing tomatoes in the same spot repeatedly—ie, by practising crop rotation.

In pots? Yes, small, bush-type cherry tomatoes are terrific in pots, but like all potted vegies they will need regular watering to do well.

Turnips

Ease of growing

Sowing time: sow seeds Apr–May in the tropics and subtropics, Jan–Apr in mild-winter areas, Jan–Mar and Aug–Oct in cold-winter areas.

Growing tips: turnips differ from swedes not only in appearance (turnips are white and smaller, swedes are beige) but also in their climate range—turnips grow well in both cool and warmer areas; whereas, swedes are best in cool regions. Turnips like a soil that was earlier enriched for a previous crop and if you sow a small batch each month of the sowing periods above, you'll get an extended harvest.

How to plant: sow seeds directly into well dug-over soil that has been broken down to a fine texture. Make shallow trenches 30–40cm apart, firm down and sow seeds thinly along them. Cover, moisten and expect germination in a week to 10 days. Thin out too-close seedlings and, as the remainder grow, thin again so that plants are 10cm apart. The second batch of thinnings can be used as turnip greens.

Routine care: keep plants moist at all times and water over monthly with liquid organic fertiliser. Remove weeds as they appear. It's normal for the tops of turnips to emerge from the soil and these should not be covered up.

Ready to pick: turnips take about three months to grow to full size but smaller roots can be harvested anytime after about eight weeks from germination. The leafy tops can be steamed and served as a green vegie or cut up and stir-fried. Turnips keep for weeks in the crisper bin of the fridge.

Watch for: caterpillars and aphids. Prevent caterpillar damage with a weekly application of Dipel or Success. Use soap spray to control aphids.

In pots? Yes, but the pot size will limit the number of turnips possible and we suggest two or three containers.

Not many zucchini varieties are sold by the major seed and seedling companies. You'll get more choice and access to heirloom varieties through the catalogues of specialist seed companies.

Zucchini

Ease of growing

Growing time: sow seeds Apr–Aug in the tropics; Jul–Oct in subtropics; Sep–Jan in mild-winter areas; Oct–Dec in cold-winter areas. Alternatively, plant bought seedlings during the same period plus one month.

Growing tips: zucchini is a highly productive plant but it takes up space—at least a square metre per plant or more. It grows best during the warmest months but, in humid areas, try to time sowing to avoid the most humid weather as plants are highly susceptible to powdery mildew. It takes about eight weeks for the first zucchini to be ready for picking and the plants keep on producing for about six weeks. Plants produce separate male and female flowers which you can identify by looking at the outside base of the flower—on female flowers there will be a tiny zucchini. If fruit does not appear to be setting, dust the centre of a male flower into the centres of several females to transfer pollen.

How to plant: sow seeds or plant seedlings in batches five weeks apart and you'll have a steady supply of zucchinis. With seeds, water in but then don't overwater—you want the soil to be lightly moist but not sodden. When seedlings emerge, gradually increase watering.

Routine care: mulch around the young plants thinly with rotted manure or compost and be sure to water them regularly. To minimise powdery mildew, direct the water at the soil rather than wet the leaves. When plants are eight weeks old, scatter a cupped double handful of chicken manure around each plant and water in.

Ready to pick: when flowering begins, the first zucchini are not far away. Look for them every day and pick when 15cm long. Don't allow the fruit to get much bigger as it loses flavour and tenderness and once fruit is 30cm or more in size, the plant stops producing. It's best to pick every day. Unopened flower buds can also be picked. Store in an airtight container in the fridge until you have enough to use.

Watch for: pumpkin beetle chews holes in leaves and fruit. Pick off and squash. Powdery mildew covers leaves with white powder. Start spraying young plants with milk solution as preventative measure.

In pots? No. Not well suited to pots as plants are too big.

Heirloom vegies

Ever since people began to grow their own food, gardeners have been saving the seeds of the superior varieties. Many of these great, old varieties are still available for you to grow. They're called heirloom or heritage vegies and they offer you a much wider choice than what you see as seeds or seedlings at the nursery.

Before there was a huge plant breeding and seed industry, gardeners would save the seeds they'd need next year from the vegies they grew this year. And because seeds are the result of the fertilisation of one plant by the pollen of another of the same type of plant, there was always the possibility that the mixing of the two plants would create a new, extra-good form of that plant.

Perhaps it had bigger or better-tasting fruit or maybe it was much more productive or resistant to a common plant disease. Whatever the improvement, our forebears recognised it as good and kept the seeds of that new, naturally 'improved' vegie.

Over the centuries, hundreds of forms of practically everything we grow to eat have been developed. But in today's world, there's not room on the shelves for every type of vegie there is, let alone for every type of known tomato, bean, pumpkin, potato or corn.

TOP LEFT: Liberty Bell peppers

TOP RIGHT: Striped eggplant

OPPOSITE PAGE: Green Oxheart tomatoes

Modern hybrids

The big seed and seedling companies only produce a small range of plants that are easy to grow and which generally give gardeners a good result. Many, but not all, of their offerings are the result of intensive breeding which produces 'F1' hybrids. These are quality plants but the seeds they produce will not lead to seedlings of the same quality. There's no point saving the seeds of 'F1' hybrids, but heirloom and heritage plants are different.

Reliable heirlooms

You can save the seeds of heirloom and heritage varieties and get great results because they are naturally pollinated. Some of the varieties sold by big seed companies are actually heirlooms, even though they don't advertise themselves as such. They're old varieties that are just so good there has been no point in trying to improve them. The parsnip 'Hollow Crown' for example, has been around since the 1800s and 'Grosse Lisse' tomatoes are an old Australian heirloom. Both are available in the Yates seed range.

OPPOSITE:
Mixed heirloom capsicums

Saving seeds

Luckily, many more of the old varieties, though harder to find, are not lost. All round the world, specialist seed companies, private organisations and even individual gardeners continue to grow old heirloom varieties and save the seed, usually because the produce tastes better than modern forms or it has some other useful advantage.

If you're keen on trying a wider range of your favourite vegies or you'd just like to try something different, it's worth seeking out suppliers of heirloom and heritage seeds. You'll be amazed at the sheer variety on offer and you're sure to be tempted by some unusual looking zucchini, strangely shaped or coloured tomatoes or some vegetable you've never even heard of.

The benefits of diversity

By growing a wider range of vegetable varieties you help to preserve the genetic inheritance of our food supply. The more types of vegies that are grown the less chance there is of a plant disease wiping out whole crops as has happened in the past—during the Irish potato famine in the 19th century, for example. Diseases can easily devastate a single genetic strain but that's much less likely if three or five or 50 different types of the one crop are commonly grown by different gardeners in the one area.

By trying a range of heirlooms you also increase the chances of discovering a variety that does really well in your soil and climate. For example, you could find a plant that's resistant to a problem you've always had with that vegie—and that kind of discovery makes vegie gardening so much easier.

Some of the sources we have listed here are heritage and heirloom seed specialists. Others are leading seed suppliers who have many heritage varieties in their range. If you're looking for a particular variety, they're well worth a visit, as they might have what you're looking for.

Heirloom or heritage seed and plant suppliers

The Digger's Club
(03) 5984 7900, www.diggers.com.au
A big range of heirloom vegetable and flower seeds.
Produces colour catalogues several times a year.

Heirloom Tomato Seed Exchange
www.heirloom-tomato-seed-exchange.net
Has many varieties of heirloom tomato seed available.

Seed Savers Network
(02) 6685 6624; www.seedsavers.net
Coordinates heirloom and heritage seed saving by private gardeners and other groups.

The Italian Gardener
www.theitaliangardener.com.au
Imports Italian vegetable seeds, many unusual varieties.

Green Harvest
1800 681 014, www.greenharvest.com.au
Heirloom, non GM, vegetable seeds and organic garden products.

The Lost Seed
(03) 6491 1000, www.thelostseed.com.au
A range of non-hybrid vegetable seeds.

Eden Seeds
(07) 5533 1107 or 1800 188 199; www.edenseeds.com.au
Includes many heirloom vegie varieties in the selection.

Greenpatch Organic Seeds
(02) 6551 4240, www.greenpatchseeds.com.au
Many heirloom vegie varieties in the selection.

Kings Seeds
(07) 4159 4882, www.kingsseeds.com.au
Some heirloom vegie varieties in the selection.

Origin Seed
(07) 4130 2722, www.originseed.com.au
Includes some heirloom vegie varieties in the selection.

Rangeview Seeds
(07) 5429 8798, www.rangeviewseeds.com.au
Includes some heirloom vegie varieties in the selection.

Royston Petrie Seeds
(02) 6372 7800; www.roystonpetrieseeds.com.au
Includes some heirloom vegie varieties in the selection.

Nurseries online
www.nurseriesonline.com.au
Find smaller growers and seed specialists here.

Overseas
Baker Creek Heirloom Seeds, Missouri, USA
http://rareseeds.com
Bountiful Gardens, California, USA
www.bountifulgardens.org
Mail-order catalogues from both. Some restrictions might apply on ordering, depending on where you are.

The best backyard fruits

Home-grown fruit is a great addition to any organic garden, but the best way to grow fruit the organic way, without the need for sprays, is to choose a plant that loves your climate zone and stays healthy, naturally.

Think small

The biggest news, the hugest news in backyard fruit tree is this: dwarfs! You can now get lots of the most popular fruit varieties in a dwarf plant. With a dwarf plant, you get full-size fruit on a half-size tree. Dwarf trees make great sense in backyards. Just look at their advantages.

1. They take up less space. Roughly speaking, dwarfs are about half the size of the 'normal' ones. So, for example, a dwarf 'Valencia' orange will reach 2m tall, while the full-size 'Valencia' orange tree is 4m tall.

2. The fruit is the same size, shape and flavour as the fruit from a full-sized tree.

BELOW: Dwarf orange 'Washington Navel'

3. Your crop will be smaller, due to the smaller tree size, and that actually helps you avoid getting that glut of too-much fruit that full-size trees usually deliver. Dwarf plants give you just the right amount of fruit each year.

4. The dwarf plant is easier and safer to get at for harvesting, as it eliminates the need for dangerous ladder-climbing.

5. Dwarf plants make your backyard bigger! Well, at least they do allow you the space to grow a couple more different fruit trees in your backyard, if you fancy the idea of a mini orchard.

6. They're also very good choices for growing in a pot.

So, the bottom line is this. Whatever fruit tree you plan on growing, have a good look at growing a dwarf variety—we love them. See our list of contacts at the end of the chapter for suppliers of dwarf plants, but there's a good chance your local garden centre has some in stock already.

Dwarf varieties available

Citrus: there are many varieties of citrus available grafted onto the dwarfing 'Flying Dragon' rootstock. From Daley's Fruit Tree Nursery, you can get dwarfs of: 'Meyer' lemon, 'Lisbon' lemon, 'Calamondin' cumquat, 'Nagami' cumquat, 'Daisy' mandarin, 'Pixie' mandarin, 'Emperor' mandarin, 'Afourer' mandarin, 'Freemont' mandarin, 'Honey Murcott' mandarin, 'Valencia' orange,

BOTTOM LEFT: Dwarf orange 'Valencia'

BOTTOM RIGHT: Dwarf Lime 'Tahitian'

'Seedless Valencia' orange, 'Washington Navel' orange, 'Lane's Late' orange, 'Cara Cara' orange, 'Hamlin' orange, 'Minneola' tangelo, 'Tahiti' lime, 'Lemonade', 'Nam Roi' pomelo, and 'Marsh' grapefruit. Dwarf citrus vary in ultimate size, depending on the species selected, from 2–3m all round. **Please note:** the 'Eureka' lemon is partially incompatible with the Flying Dragon understock. It will only live for 10–15 years on this dwarfing understock. This is only a minor problem really as most citrus trees don't live much longer than that anyway. During their slightly shortened life they still grow and fruit well. Full-sized 'Eureka' lemons also suffer a shortened life due to graft incompatibility. As well as these varieties grown on dwarf rootstocks, the kaffir lime is a naturally small-growing lime, around 1.5m tall.

Avocados: the 'Wurtz' variety, 3m tall, is the smallest avocado.

Apples: from Daley's Fruit Tree Nursery you can get dwarf 'Gala', 'Red Fuji', 'Pink Lady', 'Granny Smith', 'Red Delicious', plus low-chill 'Dwarf Dorsett Golden', 'Dwarf Tropic Sweet' and 'Dwarf Tropic Anna'. From Flemings, Trixzie 'Gala' and Trixzie 'Pink Lady' are both dwarfs about 1.5m to 2.5m high, and the slimline 'Ballerina' apples, in several varieties, are 2–4m tall but only 600mm wide.

Pears: from Flemings, the Trixzie 'Pyvert' pear marketed as Pipsqueak is 1.5m tall and wide.

Peaches and nectarines: from Fleming's Nurseries you can get 'Nectazee' miniature nectarines (1.5m tall) and the 'Pixzee' miniature peach, or a two-way graft which includes both varieties on the one dwarf tree. From Daley's Fruit Tree Nursery you can get dwarf 'Valley Red' peach, dwarf 'Sunset Dwarf Red Leaf' peach, a low-chill variety, and 'Sunset Dwarf Red Leaf' nectarine, also a low-chill variety, as well as a dwarf standard peach and a dwarf freestone peach.

Mangoes: the dwarf 'Irwin' mango is 3–7m tall.

Persimmons: non-stringent 'Ichikikijiro' is 2–3m tall.

Macadamias: Daley's Fruits stock dwarf macadamias which grow to half the size of normal macadamias.

BELOW: Dwarf peach

Citrus, the best bets

It's hard to go past citrus as a backyard fruit tree in most (but not quite all) Australian gardens. There are plenty of different citrus varieties to choose from, and we have our favourites, as we do think some citrus varieties are better bets than others for Aussie backyards.

Oranges: we love the seedless 'Valencia' orange for many reasons. The fruit has few seeds, and its juice lasts beautifully in the fridge ('Navel' orange juice goes off very quickly, by comparison, losing a lot of its flavour overnight). The fruit itself is sweeter than most other oranges, and the tree itself if fast-growing and hardy.

Lemons: for most warm and temperate areas of Australia, grow the 'Eureka' lemon. It's only in the coldest lemon-growing zones, such as chilly parts of Melbourne, that other varieties might do better. The 'Eureka' has lots going for it. It is less thorny and it crops steadily through the year. Its fruit has fewer seeds and excellent lemon flavour. Of the other lemon options, the two main ones are 'Lisbon' and 'Meyer'. The 'Lisbon' does do better in

BOTTOM LEFT:
'Valencia' orange

BOTTOM RIGHT:
'Eureka' lemon

TOP LEFT: 'Meyer' lemon

TOP RIGHT: 'Tahiti' lime

colder zones, but the tree itself is thorny, the fruit has more seeds and its cropping season is shorter. The 'Meyer' lemon is well suited to cooler climates (it's the best one for chilly zones) and as it's a smaller tree (about 2m) it does well in pots, but it has one serious drawback—it's a hybrid lemon, and so its fruit is not as 'lemony' as other lemon varieties, and its skin is also inferior in flavour, so you can't really use it grated in recipes.

Limes: the variety that's best suited to the temperate and warm climates where you can grow limes is the 'Tahiti' lime. (Limes don't like chilly zones and are not frost-tolerant.) The 'West Indian' or key lime is said to have the best flavour of all, but it can only be grown in the subtropics and tropics, it's thorny and the fruit are small. Stick with the 'Tahiti' lime, as it's the most cold-tolerant lime. The other variety worth growing is the makrut lime, also called the kaffir lime. This tree isn't really grown for the fruit—it's the 'waisted' leaves, which look like two leaves joined at the waist, that are valued in Asian cuisines. The fruit is small and knobbly, and while they produce little juice the skin has a fabulous flavour when grated and added to dishes. The kaffir lime is also a thorny plant, but if you grow it in a pot you'll get all the leaves you'll need in cooking.

Grapefruit: we recommend the red (ruby) grapefruit (eg, 'Star Ruby' or 'Rio Red') on flavour alone. It's superb, and much sweeter than the other grapefruit varieties. Grapefruit trees are larger than other citrus, around 4-6m tall.

Cumquats: this naturally smaller-growing citrus tree is one of the best citrus trees for growing in a pot. The 'Nagami' cumquat is terrific—you can eat the oval-shaped fruit straight off the tree, skin and all. In the garden this reaches 3–4m tall, but in a pot you can keep it down to 1–1.5m tall. The other good one is the calamondin, or 'Marumi' cumquat. It produces flattened fruit several times each year and with its dense, bushy growing habit it looks very handsome in a pot.

Mandarins: these are probably the best citrus for children. They can be eaten straight off the tree, and when they're good they're wonderful. The mandarin we recommend for backyards is the 'Emperor'.

How to grow citrus

All the different citrus varieties need much the same feeding and care. Provided you make a great start by choosing a variety that's well suited to your climate zone, they should give you many years of great crops. Citrus love water, food and sunshine, and they hate competition from other plants growing in their root zones. That's about it. Give them what they need and they'll do the rest for you. Here are the basics.

TOP: 'Rio Red' Grapefruit
CENTRE: 'Nagami' cumquat
BOTTOM: Mandarin

Best climates: warm, temperate spots such as the East Coast including Sydney and Brisbane, plus the West Coast from Perth northwards, plus the subtropics are all great for growing citrus. You can still grow citrus such as oranges, lemons and mandarins very well in Adelaide, Melbourne and inland areas, but the frostier your winters the more problems you might encounter. Forget about growing citrus in cold mountain zones and other very frosty climates. Up in the tropics, where it's warm year-round, the trees will look healthy but the flavour of the citrus fruit itself is sometimes disappointing, and also strange in colour, often remaining green even when ripe.

Planting times: the biggest range of citrus is usually available in autumn and early winter, but trees are available year-round. The best time to plant is either of the two mild seasons, spring or autumn. See our box on 'how to plant fruit trees' on page 257 for more planting tips.

Routine care: citrus don't care for dry spells at any time but least of all in spring and summer. As well as being big drinkers they like two good feeds a year—one in February the other in July or August. Use poultry manure (eg, Dynamic Lifter or Rooster Booster) for a purely organic diet, but lots of backyard citrus growers like to alternate feeds of citrus food (which is non-organic) and poultry manure for the other feeding. Always apply any fertiliser to moist soil and water in well afterwards.

Crop management: with any young citrus it's a good idea to remove all forming fruit and not allow any to develop the following year either. This diverts the plant's energies into more important establishment and growth. Some citrus varieties are inclined to bear heavily one year with few or no fruit the next. Mandarins and grapefruit are particularly susceptible to this alternate bearing. Train young trees out of this habit by drastically thinning overly generous crops.

Pruning: none is needed, but trees can be pruned to create a better or more useful shape or to remove a branch that's getting in your way.

Pests and diseases: fruit fly, stink bugs, scale and aphids are the usual citrus pests. See our chapter on pests and diseases for more on how to handle these pests the organic way.

Re-greening of fruit. Citrus fruit can be fully ripe and sweet even when the skin has greenish areas or the orange colour is not deep and rich. This is caused by warm night temperatures. In the tropics and subtropics, ripe citrus left on the tree can revert from orange to green when temperatures rise. The fruit is still perfectly good to eat.

Native citrus. Relatively new in our nurseries, but not new to the country, native finger limes, our own Aussie members of the Citrus genus, are an interesting bush-food citrus to try. Several different cultivars are available, including some hybrids crossed with other citrus, but the native 'finger limes' produce longish, cigar-shaped fruit which, when you cut them open, reveal tangy little spheres of citrussy flavour that look quite similar to fish roe. Plants are often quite thorny, but they're a hardy and very interesting choice in arid areas and very suitable for growing in pots. To grow them, they need similar conditions and care as other citrus.

Passionfruit

Another fruit-bearing plant which does well in many backyards is the passionfruit. This is a fast-growing climber, so it's a beaut addition to a new garden when you're looking for some instant greenery. In just a year a healthy, vigorous passionfruit vine will cover a fence or climb a pergola and start cropping for you soon after.

There are some downsides with passionfruit. One is their short lifespan. Around four to five years is normal. Another problem is that sometimes they just won't produce a crop. There are a few reasons why this might happen (see our box on 'Not Fruiting', opposite) but for most people they're trouble-free and they crop heavily. Sometimes the plants can be a bit too vigorous, smothering nearby plants.

However, passionfruit have an unforgettable flavour, they're as Australian as pavlova, and they're almost our national fruit, even though they're not a native plant. So, if you're thinking of growing passionfruit, here's the basics.

Growing passionfruit

Best climate: anywhere that's frost-free or nearly so (and the warmer the climate, the longer the fruiting season). So, you can grow passionfruit in warm parts of Melbourne or Adelaide, all the way up the East Coast and the West Coast, in the subtropics and tropics as well. If passionfruit plants are sold in local nurseries, you can grow them in your area.

Planting tips: most passionfruit sold are grafted but if you can buy an ungrafted seedling, do so (the grafted varieties tend to produce unwanted suckers at the base of the plant). The most common variety sold is 'Nellie Kelly', with the familiar black passionfruit we all know. Plant them in full sun in the most sheltered spot in your garden. Spring is the ideal planting season. Passionfruit vines are greedy feeders and always do best in deep, good quality, free-draining soil. Attach some wire mesh to a wall or fence and they'll race up that. One vine is generally enough as they can spread 3m or more either side of the planting site.

Routine care: passionfruit need a steady supply of water during the summer fruiting season (but they're not bothered by dry spells during winter). Feed plants in spring and again in summer with Dynamic Lifter (or, though it's non-organic, you can use citrus food). Apply the fertiliser beneath the entire plant and water in. If possible, keep the area under vines free of weeds, grasses and other competing plants. Though pruning is not essential, you can cut back vines anytime they get too big.

Pests and problems: fruit fly, passion vine hoppers, mealybugs and scale can attack plants. Woodiness is a disease which causes the fruit rind to become thick and the pulp dry. It also causes leaves to turn mottled yellow. There is no cure for woodiness. Plants must be pulled up and replaced. To control fruit fly, use Yates Natures Way Fruit Fly Killer or Eco-Naturalure. Natrasoap is effective against mealybugs. Use PestOil on scale insects.

> **Not fruiting?** Fruit can fail to set following spring flowers when the weather is cool. In summer, temperatures over 34°C prevent the formation of fruit. If the plant looks really healthy but bears little or no fruit, this can be due to giving plants too much fertiliser—so stop fertilising and they should come good. Excessive dryness in summer can stop fruiting, and watering over the flowers can also affect fruiting.

Strawberries

These little plants are the best backyard fruits to get your kids interested in gardening, and they can be grown in most parts of Australia except the humid tropics. They do best in the ground, but if you keep on watering them they'll thrive in pots as well.

While many strawberry varieties need some winter chills to help them set fruit, there are low-chill varieties (eg, 'Redlands Crimson', 'Redlands Joy' and 'Earlisweet') which are ideal for growing in warmer areas such as South-East Qld, where there's a major strawberry-growing industry.

Growing tips: always buy new plants from a nursery as these are certified 'disease-free'. If you plant runners dug up from a friend's existing strawberry patch, there's a good chance that they'll contain a damaging virus disease that will spoil your crop. In warm, frost-free areas, plant in March. In cooler but largely frost-free areas, plant anytime in autumn or early winter. In the coolest areas, plant in June and July. Strawberries must be grown in full sun and in soil that is rich in rotted organic matter. It must also drain freely. March-planted strawberries in the subtropics will be ready for picking in winter. Later planted strawberries mature in early and late spring, depending on when they were planted. Further flowering and crops can be expected in summer and autumn.

Routine care: keep the plants moist to establish them but reduce watering in late autumn and winter (except in areas where those times are warm). After flowering, increase watering but as fruit begins to redden, reduce watering again. From planting time, feed plants fortnightly with a liquid fertiliser such as Nitrosol, or try a 50:50 mix of Nitrosol and Seasol. Alternatively, sprinkle a small handful of Dynamic Lifter around each plant monthly. During winter, reduce the frequency of feeding to monthly or six-weekly intervals. When flowers appear, search plants often for snails or lay non-toxic, iron-based snail pellets around plants. The only pruning you'll need to do is to cut off dead leaves anytime and remove runners as soon as you see them.

Pests and diseases: aphids, snails, slugs, birds and thrips are common pests of strawberries. Grey mould is a fungus disease that often affects these plants. Use Natrasoap or Nature's Way Insect and Mite Killer against aphids and thrips but the product must be applied both under and over the leaves, onto the insects. Net plants against birds.

Short-lived Strawberry plants usually succumb to virus diseases which reduce the vigour and dramatically reduce fruit set. Plan to pull out and replace strawberries after their third summer in the ground. Plant replacement strawberries in a different spot in the garden. If using pots, scrub them clean before replanting.

How to plant a fruit tree. Some fruit trees will be sold in a pot, like any other plant. However, many deciduous varieties are sold 'bare-rooted' in winter when the plants are leafless and dormant. A bare-rooted plant will just be a few cut-back bare branches with its bare, trimmed roots wrapped in a moisture-conserving material. Here's how to plant either a potted or bare-rooted specimen.

Dig the hole: in a fully sunny but sheltered spot, dig a planting hole two to three times wider than the pot or the spread-out root system (if bare-rooted) but *no deeper* than the pot. Don't add fertiliser, compost or manure to the planting hole.

Bare-rooted plants: unwrap the roots and shake off or wash off any material from around the roots. Put the roots to soak in a bucket of water while you work. Make a mound of soil in the middle of the hole and place the plant on top, spreading the roots downwards over the soil mound. Check that the point where the trunk joins the roots is at soil level and add or remove soil from the mound until it is. The roots must be underground but barely any of the trunk should be buried. Firm soil in between the bare roots as you backfill but don't compress the soil excessively. Water in well and mulch around the plant with a 3cm-deep layer of lucerne hay or rotted cow or horse manure. Don't build the mulch up against the trunk.

Potted plants: unpot and check that roots are not curling around the base of the root-ball (straighten them out if they are, trimming if need be) and loosen the sides of the root-ball if you see a lot of roots forming the shape of the pot. Place it in the hole, making sure that the top of the potted soil is at ground level. Fill in the hole and firm down but don't compact it hard. Water in well and add more soil if slumping occurs. Mulch around the plant with a 3cm-deep layer of lucerne hay or rotted cow or horse manure.

Early care: don't apply fertiliser to either bare-rooted or potted plants until you see signs of new growth. At that point, apply fertiliser at the rate stated on the pack and water in well. Your main task with young fruit trees is to keep them steadily watered, especially during any hot spells, so they establish a good root system in their first year.

Feeding fruit trees

Fruit trees in general need a fair bit of fertiliser and water to produce a good crop, so to get a healthy, disease-free crop make sure to give your fruit trees all the food and water they need.

The most important thing when fertilising fruit trees is to apply the food to moist soil, then water in well afterwards. So, the ideal time to fertilise your fruit trees is a rainy day. The rain will water the soil beforehand for you, then it'll water in the fertiliser afterwards as well. Your neighbours might think you're a bit odd running around your garden in the rain, but your fruit trees will love you.

Fertilising is usually done in early spring and late summer. Don't apply it all near the trunk. Spread it around the area under the tree's canopy, and make sure to apply some at the very edge of the canopy (called the 'dripline' where water drips off the tree during rain) as this is where the tree's 'feeder' roots are.

There are several different plant foods to choose from, but chicken manure (eg, Dynamic Lifter or Rooster Booster) is the most popular. Lots of backyard growers also swear by citrus food, but it's not an organic plant food. Others compromise by alternating their feeding, for example applying citrus food in early spring and Dynamic Lifter in late summer. It's up to you.

Potted plants: if the plant is in a pot, feed it much more lightly

but much more frequently. Apply fertiliser monthly, scattering it thinly (or at the rate stated on the pack for the pot size you have) over the pre-moistened surface and water in.

Watering fruit trees

A steady water supply is essential for good crops of most fruits, so that means no dry spells. If it hasn't rained lately, it's time for you to water the tree. In summer, on plants which are well established in the ground, plan to apply water at least once a fortnight if good rain (25mm) has not fallen in the previous fortnight. Newly planted trees will need watering every four to five days in summer.

Potted plants: if the plant is in a pot, twice-weekly watering in summer will be needed but it's possible you'll have to water every day if the pot is on the small side and the weather is very hot. In winter, once a week will probably do but let the plant be your guide. If it wilts, give it more water. Do not sit the pot in a saucer, as sitting pots in water can cause root-rotting diseases.

Best fruits for your climate zone

Though there's a huge range of fruits you can try growing in your backyard, the easiest and best bets are citrus, strawberries and passionfruit in temperate and warm zones, and citrus and strawberries in cooler climate zones.

So, here's a run-down on what fruit trees are likely to do well in your climate zone. Please note that many other fruits are successfully grown in these climate zones, but only with a lot of care and spraying. For example, you can grow stone fruits such as peaches and nectarines in Sydney but only if you use sprays to control the many pests and diseases which bother them there.

Tropics (eg, Darwin, Cairns)
avocados, mangoes, mangosteens, passionfruit, pawpaws, pineapples, star fruit

Subtropics (eg, Broome, Brisbane)
avocados, citrus, macadamias, mangoes, pawpaws, passionfruit, pawpaws, pineapples, strawberries

Humid Temperate (eg, Sydney, East Coast)
avocados, citrus, kiwifruit, macadamias, mulberries, passionfruit, persimmons, strawberries

Mediterranean & Inland (Adelaide, Perth, Melbourne, Mildura, Canberra)
apples, blueberries, citrus, crabapples, figs, grapes, olives, persimmons, pomegranates, quinces, stone fruit (apricots, plums, peaches, nectarines), strawberries

Cool (Tasmania, mountains, NZ)
apples, blueberries, cherries, pears ('Nashi' is best in backyards), raspberries and other vine berries, stone fruit (apricots, plums, peaches, nectarines), strawberries

---

'Low-chill' varieties for warm zones. Some backyard fruit trees which some gardeners might imagine could not be grown in warmer climates now come in special 'low-chill' varieties which don't need the usual many long chilly winter nights to set good crops of fruit. For example, you can now get 'low-chill' varieties of apples, blueberries, Nashi pears, nectarines, olives, peaches, pears, plums, raspberries and strawberries.

Easiest stone fruit. Of all stone fruits, plums seem to be the least fussy about growing conditions and the least worried by pests and diseases. They don't have to be pruned (but they are improved by it) and they produce some of the sweetest and tastiest fruits of all.

Tops in pots

Some fruit trees do better in pots than others, so here's our pick of the crop for growing in pots.

Citrus: any dwarf citrus variety, plus the 'Meyer' lemon, 'Kaffir' lime, calamondins and 'Nagami' cumquats.

Figs: figs like having their roots confined in a pot, but make sure it is a big pot.

Apples: any of the dwarf varieties, plus the 'Ballerina' (narrow, columnar-shaped apples) will do well in a pot.

Stone fruits: any of the dwarf varieties, including the Pixzee dwarf peach and Nectazee dwarf nectarine, from Fleming's Nurseries.

Pineapples: you can grow pineapples from shop-bought pineapples in a pot, and they look great. The best time to do this is early spring but any time in spring or early summer will do. Cut off all the leafy top from a pineapple, with a shoulder of fruit attached. Trim the excess fruit away (it doesn't matter if some remains). Let the top dry for two days then plant it so that the lowest leaves sit at ground or potting mix level.

Strawberries: strawberries grow well in pots or hanging baskets, but you will need to keep up a steady supply of water to keep plants happy.

Olives: with their silvery-green leaves olives can look very attractive in a pot in a courtyard or on a deck.

Potting mix tip

For growing fruit trees in pots, mix together 50:50 a top quality potting mix (with the Australian Standards 'ticks' logo on the bag) and washed, coarse river sand. In Sydney we recommend the P-Coarse sand from Turtle Nurseries, but you should be able to find a similar product in all other major centres. The sand adds body to the mix, slows down the rate at which the potting mix sinks (or 'slumps') down in the pot, and helps to improve soil drainage, too.

Other good backyard fruits

Apples

ABOVE: 'Granny Smith' apples

Full-sized apple trees can be 5–8m tall, and the many apple dwarfs are half that size, or smaller. Apples are deciduous, so they're bare in winter, produce pretty blossoms in spring and crops of fruit in summer and autumn. They do best in our coldest climate zones, although new 'low-chill' varieties allow you to grow them in places like Sydney and Toowoomba now. You'll usually need to plant two trees, with one pollinating the other to produce good crops (see our box of apple pollinators, below). Apples need feeding in spring, plus a good water supply, especially through spring and summer. Crab apples are ornamental spring-flowering trees. They produce tiny, tart fruits which cannot be eaten fresh but which can be made into jams and jellies.

Apple pollinators

Gala: 'Granny Smith', 'Red Delicious', 'Red Fuji', 'Pink Lady', 'Lady Williams'.
Golden Delicious: 'Granny Smith', 'Jonathan', 'Red Fuji' and 'Red Delicious'.
Granny Smith: 'Golden Delicious', 'Pink Lady', 'Red Delicious', 'Gala', 'Jonathan', 'Lady Williams'.
Jonathan: 'Gala', 'Granny Smith', 'Golden Delicious', 'Lady Williams'.
Red Delicious: 'Gala', 'Granny Smith', 'Jonathan', 'Pink Lady', 'Red Fuji'.
Red Fuji: 'Gala', 'Golden Delicious', 'Pink Lady', 'Red Delicious'.
Pink Lady: 'Granny Smith', 'Red Delicious', 'Gala', 'Red Fuji'
Note: 'Jonathan' apples are the most popular choice used by growers to pollinate other apples.

Avocados

These large, mostly evergreen trees come in many varieties, so you should be able to find one suitable for your area—anywhere from the tropics down to warmer parts of Melbourne where temperatures don't fall below -5°C ('Bacon' is the most cold-tolerant). Avocado fruit are usually not badly affected by fruit fly, so they're potentially a good crop to grow organically. There is a dwarf variety, 'Wurtz', around 3m tall, but most avocado trees are much bigger, up to 10–12m tall. Avocados are prone to root rot diseases (phytophthora) particularly when young (apply Yates Anti-Rot to treat this). Avocado fruit does not ripen on the tree. Your best guide to ripeness is knowledge of when your variety is expected to ripen and the size of fruit. When fruit looks full size and the time is right for ripeness, cut one from the tree and let stand inside at room temperature for seven to 10 days. If it softens, pick more.

Figs

These hardy fruit trees are ideal for Mediterranean climates with cool, wet winters and warm to hot, dry summers. They don't love the humidity of the East Coast, but you'll still find plenty of fig trees growing in Sydney backyards, planted by migrant families in the 50s and 60s. They fruit in midsummer and early autumn. Figs are deciduous, so they lose their leaves in winter. They're not too fussy about soils, but they need good drainage. Their roots can be invasive, so don't plant them near buildings, paths or drains. Feed them once a year in late winter. Pruning isn't needed. Birds love to eat the fruit, so you may have to put a net over trees to preserve your crop.

Macadamias

Get a dwarf variety for a nice evergreen backyard tree, 4–7m tall with glossy green leaves. Macadamias do best in the frost-free subtropics but they're still OK to grow in Sydney or even warm parts of Melbourne. Get *Macadamia integrifolia*, with smooth leaves and shells. The other variety, *M. tetraphylla*, is prickly. Macadamias need a steady water supply.

Mangoes

These are good performers in backyards in Queensland, the Top End and around Broome, and they make a magnificent shade tree. You can still grow mangoes in Sydney and Perth, but they usually get more diseases in these cooler areas (especially anthracnose, which blackens the stems, leaves and fruits). And yes, you can grow your own from the seed of a mango bought in November or December. However, the seed must be from a 'Bowen' (aka 'Kensington Pride') or 'R2E2' mango, as most seedlings of these varieties are identical to the parent tree. Usually around four shoots come from each seed of which only one (the taller shoot in the middle) is a variable seedling, so that's the one you don't want. The other shoots are all clones, and they're the ones you want. Other named varieties of mango may not come true from seed.

Mulberries

Though not a space-saver—as it's a big tree—the mulberry is a great backyard fruit tree. As a bonus it's a super shade tree and it's also a good one for kids to climb (and feast in when fruiting). Mulberry trees grow well where winters are either cold or mild and they aren't too fussy about soils. You can grow a mulberry in a big pot but it will need regular pruning to keep it shapely and compact. There are black, white and red mulberries but the black one, *Morus nigra*, provides the best eating.

Nashi pears

These are the best backyard pear trees to grow. Fruit is crisp and juicy, more like an apple, but fairly mild in flavour when compared with the European pear varieties. Nashi pears are really good. This is probably the most garden-friendly pear variety for backyards. Look for varieties such as 'Nijisseiki' or '20th Century'. These trees are naturally self-fertile, so there's no need to plant a pollinator. They'll reach about 6–8m high and 4–5m wide.

Olives

Beautiful trees with grey-green leaves that produce their crops in late summer or autumn, these are another classic Mediterranean plant that's perfect for southern Australia, but it still does fairly well in many East Coast gardens, even though it doesn't really like the humidity there. The big thing that olive trees like is alkaline soils, so give olive trees lime or dolomite—two or three handfuls around each tree.

Persimmons

More people ought to grow these deciduous small to medium trees ('Ichikikijiro' is smaller than usual, 2–3m high). There are two types, astringent (eg, 'Flat Seedless', 'Hachiya', 'Nightingale Seedless', '20th Century', 'Dai Dai Maru') and non-astringent ('Ichikikijiro', 'Fuyu', 'Izu'). Astringent fruits cannot be eaten until the fruit is fully ripe and very soft to the touch. Non-astringent fruits can be eaten crisp when fully coloured, or allowed to soften. We prefer the non-astringent types. Persimmons need regular rainfall, but you can grow them from the subtropics down to Melbourne.

Quinces

This 4m tall deciduous fruit tree is ideal for Mediterranean climates with cool, wet winters and warm to hot, dry summers. Plant them in a sunny spot sheltered from winds (the winds can bash and bruise the fruit). Harvest the fruit in autumn. Quinces can't be eaten raw, so they need to be cooked before eating.

Pineapples

See our tips on the best bets for pots, as growing a new pineapple from a shop-bought one is fun to do. Pineapples will grow and form a fruit even as far south as Sydney and Perth. It's just that it'll take longer down south (about two years) than it will up in the tropics.

Stone fruits

Stone fruits include peaches, nectarines, apricots and plums. While there are now 'low-chill' varieties of peaches and nectarines which allow you to grow stone fruit in warmer spots such as Sydney and Toowoomba, stone fruits are at their best in cooler zones, where pests such as fruit fly are not so prevalent. These plants are deciduous, so most growers plant them in winter, when they're sold 'bare-rooted'. Stone fruit trees can make excellent specimen trees in a garden design, with their lovely spring blossoms, and the larger ones also make very good shade trees. Their downside is that they need a lot of care, a fair bit of preventative spraying each year, plus some pruning, so they're not an easy backyard fruit tree to look after. One good option is a dwarf tree, of which a good selection is available (see our section on dwarf trees for details).

Where to get fruit trees

Nurseries usually stock a range of fruit-bearing plants popular in your region. However, you can get varieties not sold locally through specialist growers, either direct or through a nursery.

Daley's Fruit Tree Nursery stocks a huge range of fruit-bearing plants including many unusual and rare tropical varieties. It is also a major producer and supplier of dwarf fruit tees and low chill varieties. Contact them at: PO Box 154, Kyogle, NSW 2474; phone (02) 6632 1441, or online at www.daleysfruit.com.au

Flemings Nursery is one of Australia's biggest wholesale growers supplying a wide range of mostly cool climate, deciduous fruit and ornamental trees to the nursery industry. They also grow and distribute dwarf nectarines, peaches and apples. Flemings is a wholesale nursery and does not sell to the public. However, your local nursery may be willing to order plants from Flemings for you. Visit www.flemings.com.au

Woodbridge Fruit Trees is an apple and pear specialist with a wide range of varieties, including dwarf trees. Contact them at: Woodbridge Fruit Trees, PO Box 95, Woodbridge, Tas 7162, or visit www.woodbridgefruittrees.com.au

Badger's Keep is a specialist in heritage apples. Contact them at: Badger's Keep, Chewton, Vic 3451; phone (02) 5472 3338; email badgers@dodo.com.au

Kendall Farms is a specialist fruit tree supplier with a wide variety of dwarf plants in its range. Contact them at: phone (07) 4779 1189, www.kendallfarms.com.au

Herbs

Set aside a bit of space in your vegie patch for herbs and you'll get lots and lots of extra flavour to add to your cooking all through the year.

Easy in pots

Most herbs are a terrific choice for pots and that's the way we like to grow most of ours—in pots. See our chapter on pots and troughs for more tips, but the main tips with growing herbs in pots are these:

• Sit the pots up on pot feet, so water drains away—don't put saucers under pots to catch water, and never let pots sit in a puddle of water.

• Use a good quality potting mix.

• If you're growing more than one type of herb in a pot, don't combine herbs that like different growing conditions. For example, basil likes plenty of water and liquid feeds, but thyme and sage like drier soils and very little feeding. See our box on 'herb teams' for good combos to try in the same pot.

Keep them handy

Wherever you end up growing herbs, make sure it's somewhere fairly close to the kitchen, so it's easy for you to pop outside into the garden and snip off enough herbs for the recipe you're cooking.

Different types of herbs

Not all herbs are the same, and so it's a good idea to know what each plant likes and dislikes. It's nothing complicated to learn, but it could make all the difference between success and failure. Here are the main differences to be aware of:

Short or long stay? First of all, some herbs will live in your garden for many years. They're in for a long stay, and they're called 'perennial' herbs. Well-known examples of perennial herbs include sage, marjoram, rosemary, thyme, mint, chives, tarragon and bay tree.

Other herbs will live in your garden for just a matter of months, after which their short stay is all over. These are the annual herbs that taste delicious, but which you'll have to keep on replanting every year. Well-known examples of annual herbs include basil, coriander and dill. Chervil and parsley both also belong in the 'short-stay' group but they are usually a bit longer-lasting than the other short-stay annual herbs.

The other thing that's important to know about some annual herbs is which growing season they prefer for their short stay. Basil, for example, loves warmth, so you should plant it during spring and early summer. Coriander, on the other hand, does much better when planted in autumn and early winter. Chervil, parsley and dill are more forgiving as to when you grow them.

Greedy feeders versus light eaters. Some herbs thrive on plenty of water and fertiliser, while others prefer very light feeds or none, and not much water, especially in summer. For example, basil, parsley and coriander love their water and food, while thyme, rosemary and sage prefer very light feeds and generally love dry summers rather than warm, humid summers. Knowing what conditions herbs like, naturally enough, means they'll be happier, but it also means that you won't make the mistake of combining two different herbs in the same pot or garden bed which prefer completely different growing conditions from each other.

Short-stay herbs

Annual herbs such as basil, parsley, dill, chervil and coriander never last all that long in the garden, and some of them such as coriander come and go in just a few months. Think of these as your 'short-stay' herbs which you'll have to replace at least once a year, sometimes more often than that.

Sowing times: basil, dill and parsley can be grown year-round in the tropics and sub-tropics, and it's only worth growing coriander there in the dry season from Sept–Mar. In temperate zones you can grow coriander at any time, but it does best from Mar-Sept, and in cool zones you can plant it from Sept–April. In temperate zones you can plant parsley and chervil from Aug–May, dill from July–Apr and basil from Aug–Mar. In cool zones you can plant parsley and chervil from Aug–May, dill from July–Apr, and basil from Sept–Feb.

Growing tips: all of these herbs grow best from seed, in well-drained, fertile soil in a sunny spot. Basil is a summer herb and must have warmth, or it won't thrive, but coriander does better in the cooler temperatures from autumn through to spring. Dill, chervil and parsley are a bit more forgiving with temperatures, and can also cope with a bit of shade during the day.

How to plant: sow repeated small crops of fast-growing, short-lived coriander and basil a couple of months apart (see seed packets for sowing depths and spacing). You'll only

BELOW: Basil

BOTTOM: Flat leaf parsley

need to replace parsley and chervil plants about once a year, and dill is somewhere in between, lasting longer than basil and coriander, but not as long as parsley. Note that parsley seed is very slow to germinate (three weeks on average) but nursery-bought parsley seedlings often don't settle in well if not well watered.

Routine care: regular watering, plus monthly liquid feeds will keep plants growing well. Regularly harvesting leaves (or trimming leaves, even if you don't need them for cooking) will help to keep plants bushy. Remove all developing flowers as you see them forming, but with all these, flowering is a signal to start planning to sow a new crop of your short-stay herbs. Chervil will set flowers fairly quickly in full sunshine, so grow it in a semi-shaded spot, and flowering will be much slower to happen.

Ready to pick: simply pick leaves of all as you need them, and if you haven't harvested leaves for a week or two, give plants a trim, anyway.

Watch for: these herbs are easy to grow and attract few pests once underway, but snails and slugs will devour small seedlings if allowed to. Hot weather will cause coriander to 'bolt' to seed, while cold weather might kill basil.

In pots? Yes, all are very suitable for growing in containers.

TOP: Dill grows best from seed.

CENTRE: Chervil prefers semi-shade.

BOTTOM: Coriander does best as a winter herb. It bolts to seed in summer.

Long-stay herbs

If they like the spot they're in, herbs such as sage, rosemary, thyme, oregano, marjoram and mint can settle in for a long and fairly easy-care life in your garden. Think of these perennials as your 'long-stay' herbs.

Sowing times: in the tropics and subtropics, you can plant oregano, mint and thyme any time of year, but start off sage in the dry season from Aug–Mar, and don't bother trying to grow rosemary there at all. In temperate zones you can plant oregano and mint from Jul–April, thyme and sage from Aug–Mar, and rosemary any time you like. In cool zones, plant oregano and mint from Aug–Mar, rosemary from Sept–May and thyme and sage from Sept–Feb.

Growing tips: sage, oregano, rosemary and thyme are all Mediterranean herbs that like sunshine, well-drained soils, wet, cool winters and hot, dry summers, so aim to give them these conditions if you can. All four of these Mediterranean herbs need only very light feeding with a slow-release fertiliser applied in spring, but they do grow and look better if you cut them back regularly. Mint is different—it likes moisture all-year-round and monthly liquid feeds and does better in semi-shade. Mint also must be contained in a pot, or it will spread rapidly and take over your garden beds.

How to plant: while seed is available for these plants, most people grow them from

TOP: Sage thrives in the summer heat.

CENTRE: Rosemary can be clipped into a hedge.

BOTTOM: Thyme makes a good, low groundcover.

seedlings bought at a nursery, or by taking cuttings of established plants (rosemary and mint are especially easy to strike from cuttings). Usually one plant of each is all you'll need for cooking.

Routine care: cutting back plants, whether you need leaves for cooking or not, will help to make them all grow into a bushier, better looking form. Mint needs lots of water, daily in summer, plus the occasional major cutback to tidy it up if it gets straggly. If your winters are dry, give your oregano, sage, rosemary and thyme the occasional good soaking, but don't water them much in summer, especially if you are on the moist, humid East Coast, where these plants can struggle during a wet, humid summer.

Ready to pick: just pick leaves anytime you need them, and if you haven't harvested leaves for a few weeks, give plants a trim, anyway.

Watch for: once established, all of these long-stay herbs are relatively pest-free. Wet weather in summer, combined with poorly drained soils, can make oregano, sage, thyme and rosemary look poorly.

In pots? Yes, all are well suited to pots, but give oregano and thyme a wide, shallow pot to spread in, and give sage and rosemary a big pot (40cm diameter or more). Always grow mint in a pot.

TOP: Oregano spreads quickly.

CENTRE: Marjoram has a flavour similar to oregano.

BOTTOM: Mint should be grown in a pot.

Herb teams

Some herbs get on better with other herbs because they like the same growing conditions, so try these teams together in either the same pot, or the same spot in a garden bed.

Dry team herbs
Sage, thyme, marjoram, oregano, rosemary
1: Rosemary grows the tallest, so plant it at the back; sage is the next biggest, so it goes towards the back, too.
2: Thyme is the smallest, so it goes at the front. Both marjoram and oregano will spread like a groundcover, so plant them near the edges of the pot.
3: All these herbs only need a light feeding of slow-release food (eg, Osmocote) in spring.
4: Don't over-water these in summer. They all prefer a wet cool winter and a warm to hot and dry summer.
5: You'll need a very big pot to hold all of these plants, so maybe just choose a few for one pot.

Greedy team herbs
Parsley, basil, dill, chives
1: All of these herbs like monthly liquid feeds, plenty of sunshine and a steady supply of water.
2: They all grow to roughly the same size, but put taller-growing basil at the back of the pot or bed.

Mint—not a team player!
1: Mint is not good at sharing space in pots and will take over, so plant it on its own.
2: Mint prefers semi-shade, while other herbs like sun, and it also needs lots of water—and the only other herb which likes those conditions is… more mint!

Other herbs to try

Bay leaves: a fully grown bay tree planted in the ground can reach 10m or more tall—it's a big tree—so plant a bay tree in a big pot to keep its size under control. Bay trees like sunshine and a steady water supply, plus feeds with slow-release fertiliser in

spring. They can be attacked in winter by scale insects, but regular sprays with Pestoil can control that sucking insect problem.

Tarragon: this liquorice-flavoured perennial herb tastes great with chicken, but the trick with it is to grow only the French tarragon (*Artemisia dracunculus*). The other types (ie, Russian tarragon and Mexican tarragon) have a poor flavour by comparison. Buy only seedlings of French tarragon, which are grown from cuttings. Any seed labelled as 'French' tarragon or just 'Tarragon' is more likely to be the Russian or Mexican type as true French tarragon hardly ever sets seeds. Where winters are cool to cold, tarragon dies back in winter, but it will bounce back in spring.

Garlic: garlic is classed as a herb and is well worth growing. Plant individual cloves 3–5cm (1–2 inches) deep in well-drained soil in a sunny spot in autumn or early winter, and it will grow into a hand of garlic by the next summer. (You'll know it's ready to harvest when the tops of the plant start to die back). While garlic does best in cooler climates, there are so many garlic varieties to try that you should be able to find one suited to warmer zones, if that's where you live.

Trim, trim, trim!

If you haven't needed to use any herbs lately in your cooking, the plants outside in the garden can become scrappy looking. The solution is simple—give the plants a trim and they will grow more bushy again. All

TOP: Bay leaves on bay tree
CENTRE: French tarragon
BOTTOM: Garlic

herbs love being trimmed, and all will benefit from a cutback. Mint, for example, can get very leggy and scrappy at times. Give it a major cutback (see our photos of our mint pot cutback, below) and it will take only a couple of weeks to be looking fabulous again. The same applies to potted chives, which can become tangled and scrappy looking if ignored for several weeks, but it's true for virtually all other herbs as well. Give them a trim!

Mint pot cutback
TOP LEFT: Mint before pruning

TOP RIGHT: Cutting the mint, you can prune it right back

BOTTOM LEFT: The mint looks dead immediately after pruning, but give it a liquid feed

BOTTOM RIGHT: Just 18 days later, the mint has regrown and is ready to use

Problem solving
pests and diseases

Safe pest control

When you grow vegies the organic way, you will almost certainly suffer a few losses due to pests such as caterpillars or even to your local birds; but you can still control many pests and diseases without harming your crops or your health.

Driving them off takes a two-pronged strategy. First, identify the culprits then choose one of the several safe, organic remedies available today.

One of the main reasons we like to grow our own vegies organically is that we know for sure that the crops are clean, healthy and uncontaminated. So that means we don't want to use harmful poison sprays. That's a great idea because it's a fact that residues of poisonous insecticides found in food can affect our health. The trouble is, it's also a fact that the crops we grow are attractive to damaging insects and they're also vulnerable to a number of plant diseases.

Egg hunt. While you're looking on and under leaves for pests, keep an eye out for insect eggs. If you see tiny clusters like these, rub them off and you can stop a problem before it even hatches.
Of course, it won't be a permanent solution. There'll be more the next day or the day after but once you're familiar with what's normal and what's not on your crops you'll be surprised how many pests infestations you can stymie with your thumb and forefinger.

Regular patrols

For a start, be vigilant and go on regular patrols around your vegie garden. Get into the habit of looking at your vegies every day. If you don't want to use poison sprays, become the garden's guardian. An insect infestation always starts out in a minor way and if you see the first signs of damage it's likely you could find the culprit there and then. It might be hidden under the leaves or have moved to a nearby plant. If you find it, squash it. Problem solved, no other treatment needed.

Whodunnit?

Sometimes though, hand control just won't work – some insects and bigger pests do their damage at night. That's when you have to resort to an applied remedy. But before you can know what to spray, you have to know what's causing the problem. It could be an insect, an animal such as a rat or possum, or a plant disease.

Insects cause damage in one of two ways. They either suck sap or chew holes. Sap-sucking can cause wilting or distortion, deformation, spotting, streaking, discolouration or fruit fall. Chewing insects make holes in leaves or stems or fruits, but rats and possums will also chew holes, usually fairly big holes, or they may devour the plant to the ground.

Diseases are less common than insects and usually cause spotting, rotting, yellowing and/or wilting. Diseases don't cause big holes to suddenly appear in fruit or leaves.

Common garden pests

Chewers	Suckers	Other
Beetles	Aphids	Ants – ants often spread and protect sucking insects like aphids and scale insects.
Borers	Bugs, ie sucking insects	Gall wasps – vey small, so not noticed; galls (swelling in stems) are easily seen.
Caterpillars	Mites	-
Fruit flies (maggots)	Planthoppers	-
Grasshoppers	Scale	-
Grubs	Thrips	-
Katydids	Whiteflies	-
Leafminers	Mealybugs	-
Sawflies	-	-
Slugs	-	-
Snails	-	-
Curl Grubs	-	-
Weevils	-	-
Locusts	-	-
28 spot ladybird	-	-

Good guys

Not every insect in your vegie patch is trying to rob you. Some are your friends, drawn to the vegies by the other insects there. These are the predatory insects which happily devour the sap-suckers and leaf-chewers. They can help control the problem for you. The good guys include:

Ladybirds (all types, other than 28 spot ladybird)
Spiders (not true insects)
Assassin bugs
Praying mantises
Lacewings
Dung beetles
Predatory wasps

Buy a bug! You can buy predatory mites, lacewings and other beneficial insects for your garden online – check out these Australian companies:
www.bugsforbugs.com.au
www.goodbugs.org.au
www.bugcentral.com.au

Friends and foes

Curl grubs

You'll probably come across these when you're digging over the vegie patch prior to planting. Curl grubs are the larvae of various scarab beetles, including black African lawn beetles. They mostly live on organic matter in the soil but they'll also eat plant roots and, in large numbers, can cause newly-planted seedlings to remain stunted or to wither and die.

Controlling curl grubs: the safest control method is to simply squash them as you uncover them or, if there are chooks, magpies or currawongs around, toss the grubs to them.

Caterpillars

Caterpillars are the larval stage of moths or butterflies. They hatch out from eggs laid by the adult moth or butterfly and spend the next few weeks fattening themselves up by gorging on leaves, flowerbuds or by tunnelling into stems and fruits (depending on the type of caterpillar). When fully fed, they spin

TOP LEFT: curl grubs eat roots. They are beetle larvae and are quite common.

TOP RIGHT: caterpillars are baby moths and butterflies and come in many sizes and colours.

themselves a cocoon and transform from a grub into the adult moth or butterfly.

In vegie patches, caterpillars can do great damage to almost everything you'd want to grow. They are a serious pest of leafy vegetables and can also ruin tomatoes and other crops. These holes, pictured, are typical damage caused by caterpillars and you'll also see clusters of their droppings. The bigger the individual droppings, the bigger the caterpillar. For hand control, closely examine both surfaces of the damaged leaves and nearby leaves.

The cabbage white butterfly is one of the most common pests of vegies. When you see this butterfly flitting around the vegie patch, damage from its green caterpillars will soon be seen. Its favourite food plants are Chinese greens (pak choy etc), cabbages and Chinese cabbages, broccoli, Brussels sprouts and cauliflower.

Cabbage white butterflies flit from leaf to leaf, alighting on each for only a few seconds. When you see the butterfly land, examine the leaf for its tiny yellow eggs. Squash there and then. Some people suggest laying white half chicken eggshells around the vegie garden to repel the adult butterflies. The theory is that the eggs look like white butterflies laying eggs, so the real butterflies lay their eggs elsewhere.

TOP LEFT: caterpillars can make a mess of your vegies.

TOP RIGHT: the cabbage white butterfuly attacks cabbage family plants quite often.

BELOW: look on the underside of leaves for insect eggs.

Safe caterpillar sprays: all caterpillars can be controlled with either Success or Dipel. Neither spray product is a poison. Both are based on naturally-occurring bacteria which only affect caterpillars. Even if a bird later eats an infected caterpillar, the treatment has no effect on the bird. Spray susceptible plants thoroughly when damage is first seen. Neither Success nor Dipel lasts more than a few days so frequent re-application is necessary. You can spray all your vegies with these products as a safe, preventative measure.

Ladybird beetles

Most ladybird beetles are great friends of gardeners. In both their larval and adult stages they eat a range of other pest insects, notably aphids, and some species even eat the white, powdery mildew from the leaves of zucchini, pumpkins and melons. But a few ladybird beetles are not predators. They eat leaves and can do considerable damage.

The goodies: most ladybird beetles are carnivores and therefore good. One of the goodies is the yellow and black, fungus-eating ladybird beetle. It congregates on the leaves of plants blighted with powdery mildew, where it busily eats the fungus.

The larval stage of the fungus-eating ladybird beetle is also an efficient consumer of mildew. Don't spray or squash these good

BOTTOM LEFT: Ladybirds eating powdery mildew are helping the organic gardener.

BOTTOM RIGHT: Powdery mildew also affects peas. It looks like its name implies: white powder on leaves.

friends. Another good ladybird beetle controls mealybugs, which are a very nasty pest. The ladybird mealybug predator (*Cryptolaemus*) can be purchased by mail-order from Bugs for Bugs. (This company also sells a scale insect predator, *Chilocorus*, an orange-coloured ladybird. See the website at www.bugsforbugs.com.au)

The baddies: of the leaf-eating ladybirds, the 28-spot labybird beetle is most commonly encountered. It's fairly big for a ladybird but it can be confused with the beneficial 18-spot ladybird so don't take action unless the beetle is in damaging numbers and you can clearly associate it with damage.

The larval stage is yellowish with dark spines. It too consumes leaves but, unlike the adult, which mostly feeds on the upper surface, the larva of the 28-spot ladybird beetle mostly feeds on the undersides.

Controlling ladybirds: squashing the larval and adult stages by hand is the only truly organic control method. For heavy infestations, spraying with pyrethrum will control this beetle. Pyrethrum has a very low toxicity to humans and other animals but, to be effective, you must spray the beetle or its larvae directly. It only lasts about a day on the plant and does not get inside the plant tissue. But remember, these sprays will also kill the far more common beneficial ladybirds.

BOTTOM LEFT: This leaf-eating ladybird is not an organic gardener's friend.

BOTTOM RIGHT: These are the larvae (babies) of the leaf-eating ladybird. If you see them (and they are tiny) get rid of them.

Pumpkin beetle

Orange and black pumpkin beetles attack the flowers and leaves of pumpkins, melons, zucchini and squashes. They are most serious on young, small plants as they can easily devour them to the ground. The most commonly seen damage is holes in leaves but the beetle will also gnaw at the skin of pumpkins, causing minor damage.

Controlling pumpkin beetle: they are easy to pick off and squash by hand and this is the best and safest organic control measure. Low-toxicity pyrethrum sprays, as described under ladybird beetles, are also effective if sprayed directly onto the insects.

Aphids

Aphids are sap-sucking insects which cluster together in colonies on new shoots or under new leaves, usually along the centre vein. Each aphid is barely bigger than a pinhead but they occur in vast numbers. They can cause shoot tips to wilt and die or young fruits to fall early. They can also transmit plant diseases. Aphids are a favourite food of ladybird beetles and their young but unless there are a lot of them about, don't rely on them to control big numbers of this fast-breeding pest.

Controlling aphids: squash by hand or spray with Yates Nature's Way Insect and Mite Killer. This product is based on spinosad, a naturally-occurring bacterium. It is harmless to humans, pets and garden wildlife. Alternatively, erect a sticky yellow trap. These are sheets of board that are coloured bright yellow and coated with a non-drying glue. The yellow colour attracts aphids and also whiteflies which stick fast to the glue. On the downside, these traps (which also come in blue for thrips and fungus gnats) attract many other insects as well so they do considerable damage to non-target insect populations.

Sticky traps. You can buy sticky traps to control aphids and whiteflies from some large garden centres, but if you're having trouble finding them locally, online you can mail-order them from Green Harvest (www.greenharvest.com.au). They're in the Garden Pest Control shop, priced around $1.50 each.

Snails and slugs

The best organic way to control snails and slugs is to go on patrol for them regularly, and get to know their hide-outs – usually cool, shady and moist spots. You might find them under pot rims, underneath steps or garden seats, or at the base of thickets of plant stems. They'll always be most active during wet weather, so that's the ideal time look for them. You should also look after your blue-tongued lizards, as they mostly eat snails.

Controlling snails & slugs: go out on regular patrols, especially in wet weather, and when you find them, squash them with your shoe. A beer trap is another popular method, simply set a small bowl of beer into your garden, low enough for snails to get in. They are attracted to the beer, fall in and drown. Putting out snail pellets isn't the organic way, but some snail pellets are better

environmentally than others. Multiguard pellets are based on iron and at least they won't harm your pets, native birds or lizards, if they eat them. We've tried using 'organic' snail barriers such as crushed eggshells, coffee grounds, blood and bone, and cat litter, and found none of them worked well. However, snails react badly when they come in contact with copper, so laying copper wires around garden beds can help to keep snails out.

And if you're thinking of keeping some ducks, a big bonus for vegie gardeners is that ducks love to eat snails and so your snail problems will be solved forever!

Nematodes

These are very tiny worm-like pests that cause swellings in the roots of plants. Tomatoes, Chinese gooseberries, potatoes and many other plants are attacked. Often you get lumps on the plants' roots. Marigolds (*Tagetes*) do repel nematodes or you could rotate your crops with nematode-resistant ones.

Fruit fly

These are a serious pest of fruit and other crops, notably tomatoes, in many parts of Australia, especially our warmer regions. Fruit fly lay eggs into fruit, ruining the fruit as the larva hatches into a grub and starts eating the fruit from within. If you live in an area where fruit fly are known to exist, they'll almost certainly attack your crops during summer.

Controlling fruit fly: fortunately, there are organic control options for fruit fly. One is to protect individual fruits or branches with 'exclusion bags' which keep fruit fly out but allow light and air to circulate. These are available from organic gardening suppliers such as Digger's Seeds (www.diggers.com.au) and Green Harvest (www.greenharvest.com.au) but some larger garden centres will stock them, too. Several different sizes and styles of bag are made, so you should find some to suit your particular fruit crop.

New fruit fly sprays are now available, based on Spinosad, a bacteria that affects the flies. These are sold as concentrates which you mix up with water, then spray according to the packet directions. Two leading brands are Yates Nature's Way Fruit Fly

Killer, and Eco-Naturalure. Being organic, the spray has to be applied repeatedly, and again after rain, so it's a fair bit of work to keep up the spray program, but it works.

Grasshoppers

Grasshoppers are chewing insects which do most of their damage after dark. They can do a lot of damage quickly, tearing big holes in leaves and also damaging the crop itself. Grasshoppers can be green or brown or a combination of these colours but all have long feelers attached to their heads and will spring away quickly if disturbed. There are several different types and they can be anything from a little over 1cm long up to 5cm or more long. The more severe the damage and the quicker it occurs, the bigger the grasshopper.

Controlling grasshoppers: there is neither an organic spray nor a poison home gardeners can use with confidence against grasshoppers. The pests are mostly a problem later in summer and in autumn and, as they are least active and easiest to catch when temperatures are low, a good strategy is to get up early and catch the critters between your fingers. Alternatively, use a butterfly net. We have heard it claimed that grasshopper juice sprayed over plants is an effective deterrent. To make it, mash a number of grasshoppers and mix the mash with water. Strain then spray over infested plants. It might work. Another method is to float pieces of bright yellow plastic in a bowl of water. The insects are attracted to yellow but cannot get out of the water. Fine mesh laid over vulnerable plants will exclude grasshoppers, but, of course, there must be no grasshoppers on the plants when you cover them.

Citrus pests.

Citrus gall wasp: if you see a strange looking lump developing inside a citrus stem, that's the work of the citrus gall wasp. This pest is easy to control organically. This tiny wasp lays its eggs into the stems of citrus trees in spring. As the wasp eggs hatch and the grubs feed on the stem tissue, the branch swells. All you have to do is cut off the affected stems before the grubs inside emerge as wasps. Collect all the cut pieces and either burn them or seal them tightly inside a plastic bag. By destroying the grubs inside the stems you will prevent re-infestation by the adult wasps.

Stink bugs: these get their name from the smelly, caustic fluid they squirt when disturbed. This is dangerous, especially if it gets in your eyes, so always wear eye protection. Stink bugs suck sap, causing new shoots to wilt and brown. They also cause young fruits to drop before they ripen. They first appear in late September as small, oval-shaped, translucent green insects with a darker dot on their backs. As they grow they turn orange and it's at this stage you normally notice them. While in the orange stage they are too young to reproduce so that is the ideal time to control them. You can use a gloved hand to knock them into a bucket of water with a little kero added. Some people use a vacuum cleaner to remove them (but the vile smell will permeate the appliance's filters so only use an old machine). Pyrethrum sprays also kill them, but remember that these sprays can also kill good guys such as bees and ladybirds, so take care. Fully mature stink bugs are black and shield-shaped.

Spined citrus bugs: these are green, shield-shaped bugs with a spine on each shoulder. They attack citrus fruit, causing brown, dry patches in the fruit and some early fruit fall. Treat them as for stink bugs.

Leaf miner: this is a tiny caterpillar which burrows between the upper and lower surfaces of new leaves, causing wiggly, silvery trails in the leaves. The leaves also curl up and deform so severe infestations can look bad. Just cut off any damaged leaves if the look bothers you, but you can ignore this pest if you like, as the damage it does is not severe.

Scale insects: there are several different types of scale but all are immobile and appear in numbers on leaves or stems. Scale can look like desiccated coconut or tiny brown blobs or it may be white and waxy, or pink and waxy. You can scrape scale off with a fingernail and beneath the outer covering lives the sucking insect. PestOil is effective against scale (it smothers them). Alternatively, wipe small infestations from leaves or use a toothbrush and soapy water to scrub scale from trunks and stems.

Possums and rats

Both possums and rats can do considerable damage in the vegie patch. Possums will eat both succulent foliage and ripening fruits whereas rats normally stick to fruits. Tomatoes are one of their favourites.

Both possums and rats will chew large holes in near-ripe tomatoes. If possums are the culprits, usually you'll also find damage to leafy vegies such as lettuce and parsley as well as damage to ornamental plants

such as roses, grapevines and New Zealand Christmas bush. Continental parsley is another favourite of possums who will eat them down to ground level.

Controlling rats and possums: you can lay baits or traps for rats but be especially careful if you have dogs, which will be attracted to the bait. There are dog-proof rat traps available at hardware stores but it is still best to keep dogs inside when rat baits or traps are in use overnight. Remove them during the day.

Possums are a protected native animal and may not be trapped or harmed in any way. A physical barrier, such as a wire mesh enclosure (for example, the guinea pig mesh Matt and Luke used on their vegie garden – see page 97) is the only sure way to prevent possum damage. We have not found any of the commercial or home-made possum repellents to be reliably effective and most have to be applied virtually daily. Other people have recommended a spray made of wasabi (the hot, Japanese paste) and water, which the possums apparently don't like. Others say possums don't like black tea, so spray around a superstrong brew and see how that goes.

ABOVE: The bigger the pest the greater the damage done. A possum can eat a lot in one night.

RIGHT: This garden has been posssum-proofed with low wire mesh cages.

Birds

All sorts of birds, both native and non-native, love to eat fruit, so you might find them feasting on your crops just as they are becoming ripe. First of all, remember that native birds are all protected species under law, so it's illegal to harm them. Your only option is to keep them off your crops. But do also remember that many birds are terrific insect-eaters, and they'll eat a lot of pests that might otherwise munch on your crops, so adopting a 'live and let live' policy might be the easiest and best approach.

Controlling birds: you can buy nets to drape over fruit trees to keep the birds out, and these can work well if the tree isn't too big. You could also build a scarecrow to protect crops, but once the birds get used to the scarecrow never moving, they'll figure out that he's nothing to worry about. One really great option is to build an 'anti-aviary'. What's that? Well, it's just like an aviary that people have to keep birds in, but an 'anti-aviary' keeps birds out. Build a frame around and over your vegie patch then cover it with wire, to keep birds out. Make it big enough so you can stand up in it, and add a good gate. Bird problem solved forever. Sure it costs more, but it's a good, permanent solution. In country areas or near bushland, where birds can be a major nuisance, vegie gardeners should seriously consider an anti-aviary.

Another option which has had great success is the Hawk Bird Scarer sold by Tisara Australia, phone (02) 4934 8330, or visit www.hawkbirdscarer.com. On a similar vein we've heard of people having success with everything from setting up a realistic plastic owl through to a well-made, realistic statue of a kookaburra. The kooka statue sits there, just like a real kookaburra does.

If ducks are your problem, leaving out the garden hose to look like a snake or, better still, pieces of old garden hose like a few snakes, could do the trick.

> **Working birds.** One important bonus of keeping chooks, apart from the eggs and the wonderful personalities, is your chooks will earn their keep by eating a wide variety of insects that would otherwise munch on your crops. And if you keep ducks, your slug and snail problems will be over.

Dogs

If your dog is proving to be a major pest in your vegie patch, there's only one way to keep it out and that's to effectively fence it off and teach the dog that it's a no-go zone. A chainwire-enclosed area is perfect for growing climbing peas, beans or passionfruit, so you create a living fence.

Heat damage

Sometimes damage is not caused by any sort of living thing. These bean leaves (below) couldn't cope with a 40°C day so when it's exceptionally hot you may find similar damage on many types of plant. Don't do anything. New leaves will form and, in the meantime, the damaged leaves are providing some shade to the plant, should another hot day strike.

Diseases

Fertile, free-draining soil and control of sap-sucking insects is your best defence against plant diseases yet even so, plants can become infected. Disease can be caused by a fungus of one sort or another or by bacteria or viruses. Organically, there's not much you can do against diseases, and if plants start to seriously suffer, prompt removal and off-site disposal is the best course.

Don't replant the same crop or any of its relatives in that spot for at least two years.

Milk spray, which is one part milk in nine parts water (for 500mL, mix 50mL milk into 450mL water) is reasonably effective against powdery mildew but only if you apply it every day or two, starting from the moment the first spots of white mildew are seen. It is less effective when the leaf is heavily infected with mildew. It seems that full-cream milk is best.

Copper-based fungicides such as Yates Fungus Fighter or Kocide, though not strictly organic, are based on copper, a fungicide which has been in use for centuries. Copper sprays are effective against various leaf spotting diseases.

Seaweed extracts, such as Seasol, can strengthen plants' natural resistance to diseases. To be effective, it has to be sprayed over all leaves every two weeks from the time you plant. It is not a curative, more a preventative. Growing disease-resistant varieties of vegies is often the best solution. For example, cherry tomatoes are usually far more pest and disease resistant than full-sized tomatoes.

Tomatoes are particularly susceptible to plant diseases, the symptoms of which are leaf spotting and yellowing and the death of leaves, usually starting at the bottom of the plant and working upwards. The odd lower leaf turning yellow is not a problem as that is what happens as plants grow taller. Diseases make the bulk of the plant look unwell, not just a few leaves. This is bacterial canker in tomato. Affected plants should be removed and burned or taken to the tip.

Companion planting

This is a popular idea – creating 'teams' of plants which help each other in various ways (or, alternatively, sometimes it means avoiding certain combos of plants which don't get on well with each other in the garden).

Probably the best-known companion planting team is to grow marigolds (*Tagetes*) in your vegie patch. The marigolds help the vegies because they reduce nematode populations in soils, and they also repel whitefly when grown near tomatoes. The next best-known 'team' is basil and tomatoes (the basil helps to repel insects from the tomatoes).

The sad fact is that there is little scientific evidence to show that companion planting works. But it's a nice idea, it does no harm and who knows, one day scientists might be able to prove that it works! If you want to give it a go, try these classic companion planting combos, and a few companion planting no-nos:

Grow carrots with chives, leeks, onions, peas, lettuce and sage.
Grow cabbage with potatoes and sage.
Grow peas with sweet corn.
Don't grow peas with garlic, onions or shallots.
Don't grow pumpkins with potatoes.

Growing your own organic food and keeping a few chooks is incredibly satisfying and fun and is something the kids will remember forever.

Not only will it save you money, you'll also be able to enjoy chemical-free produce, do your bit for the planet and enjoy the best vegies you've ever tasted.

I hope we've inspired you.

Go forth and have a go at growing your own organic food. If you enjoy it half as much as I do, it will be one of the most rewarding experiences of your life.

Don.

Index

abuse of organics 18
ACO (Australian Certified Organic) 19
ACQ (Alkaline Copper Quaternary) treated pine 30
animal manures 14, 17, 29, 32
aphids **288**
apples **112**, **262**
    apple pollinators 262
    dwarf varieties 249
    early season 112
    late season 112
    mid season 112
aquaponics 197-8
Araucana **168**
archways 31
Artemisia dracunculus 276
artichokes **204**
Asian greens **104**, *145*, 194, **205**
Asian spices **206-7**
asparagus **207-8**
Australian Government Analytical Laboratories (AGAL) 13, 14
Australian Pesticides and Veterinary Medicines Authority (APVMA) 11
Australian Quarantine Service (AQIS)
    National Standard for Organic and Biodynamic Produce 19
Australorp 160, 161, **164**
autumn planting 85-99
    plan 92-3
    preparation 85-7
    7 weeks after planting 95
    14 weeks after planting 98
avocados 249, **263**

Bacillus thuringiensis 17
bananas 109
Barnevelder **168**
basil 45, 179, 270, 271, 275
bay tree 270, 275-6
beans 45, **115**, 147, 151, 194, **208-9**
    planting 47
beetroot *54*, *58*, 91, **106**, 146, 180, 181
biodynamics 18
Biological Farmers Association (BFA) 13, 14, 19, 32
birds 177, 295
    controlling 295
Black Australorp Cross **164**, 195
block planting 48
blood and bone 13
bok choy 54, 84, **104**, 181, 192, **205**
bottling 118-19
Brama Bantam **169**
bread rolls with pesto and oven-dried tomatoes 83-4
broad beans 91, **107**, 174, *180*, 181, *182*, **209**
    support 97
broccoli 94, *96*, 181, **210**
Brussels sprouts 94, 181, **211**

bug collecting 154
Burke's Backyard 8, 13
bush peas 88

cabbages 94, *96*, 174
capsicums 45, **107-8**, 146, 194, **214**
carrots 91, *98*, **106**, 146, 151, 181, **212**
Carson, Rachel
    Silent Spring 11
caterpillars **284-6**
cauliflower 94, **212-13**
chemicals 10-11, 14
chervil 270, 271, 272
chickens *see* chooks
children 50, 151-4, 192-3
    bugs, collecting 154
    flowers 153
    plants for beginners 151
chillies 146, 194, **214**
Chinese broccoli **104**, 145, **205**
Chinese cabbage 94, **108**, 145, *181*, **205**
Chinese chard 84, 181, **104**, 145, **205**
chives 179, 270, 275
Chlordane 10, 11
chocolate zucchini cake 69
chook house 162, 195
chooks 157, 189, 295
    benefits 158
    breeds 158, 164-9, 195
    buying 170
    choosing 159, **164-9**
    crossbred egg layers 160
    feeding 162
    housing 162
    layer hens 159
    meat chooks 160, **169**
    purebred egg layers 160
    purebred ornamental 160
    types 160-1, **164-9**
choy sum **104**, 181, 192, **205**
chutneys 119
citrus **113-14**, 151, 250-3
    dwarf varieties **248-9**
    growing 252-3
    native 254
    pests **292-3**
    potted 147-8
    regreening of fruit 253
citrus gall wasp **292**
clay soil 25, *25*
    compost and 124-5
climates 36, 259-60
climber clips 88
climbing peas 88
Cochin **168**
companion planting 195, 297
compost 24, 123-35, 183, 196
    aerated bins 131
    air 132-3

299
Index

benefits 123-6
bins 127-31, 183
clay soil 124-5
cost 126
DIY compost tumbler 138-9
dry ingredients 133-4
liquid fertiliser 126
location 128-9
materials to put in 131-2
moisture retention 124
mulch 126
potting mix 126
sandy soil 124-5
size 132
smell 134
time 134
tumbler bins 129-30, *183*
turning 129, 134
vegetable gardens and 125
wet ingredients 133
construction of organic vegetable garden 23-32
   finishing touches 31-2
   ground preparation 27-9
   layout *32*
   raised edges, building 30
   soil 24-5
containers 40-1, 141-8
   drainage holes 142-3
   feeding 144-5
   fruit trees 147-8, 261
   material 142
   plants 145-7
   pot feet 143
   potatoes 148
   potting mix 144
   setting up 143
   site 143
   size 142
   strawberries 14
   watering 145
cool climate 260
cool-season crops 35
   planting times 36
   preparation 85-7
   renovating beds 85
coriander 179, 270, 271, *272*
corn 45, 48, *57*, 60, **114**, 146, 151, **215**
country garden 187-98
Crean, Simon 11
cucumber **104**, **216**
cumquats 148, 252
   dwarf 248
   'Nagami' *252*
curl grubs **284**
curry-leaf tree *179*

DDT 10-11, 14
Dieldrin 10, 11
Digger's Seeds 194

dill 179, 270, 271, *272*, 275
Dipel 96, 182
diseases 296-7
DIY compost tumbler 138-9
dogs 296
dolomite 17, 182
drying foods 120-1
dwarf fruit trees 247-9
Dynamic Lifter 29, 30, 32, 147, 196, 255, 256

edging *28*, 30
eggplant 45, *55*, *59*, *60*, 146, 194, **217**
eggplant parmigiana 70
Endrin 11
English spinach 181, **232**

fertilisers, organic 13, 17, 182
   compost *see* compost
figs 148, **263**
finger limes 252
Fowler Vacola 118
French marigolds 48, *57*
Frizzles 161, **166**
fruit fly 45, **290-1**
fruit trees 181, 247-67
   citrus *see* citrus
   climate zones 259-60
   dwarf 148, **247-9**
   feeding 258-9
   planting 257-8
   potted 147-8, 261
   stone fruit 260
   suppliers 267
   warm zones 260
   watering 259
fungicides 48

gai lan **104**, **205**
galangal **206-7**
garden blog 185
gardens
   country 187-
   small 175-85
garlic **114**, 181, **276**
ginger **206-7**
gluts 37
grapefruit 252
   dwarf 249
   'Rio Red' *252*
grapes 147, **218-19**
grasshoppers **291**
greenhouses 193-4
ground preparation 27-9
growth of spring plants
   3 weeks after planting 54-5
   4 weeks after planting 56-7
   6 weeks after planting 58-9
   11 weeks after planting 60
gypsum 17, 29, 32

harvest and storage 103-17
heat damage 296
heirloom vegetables 7-10, 192, 239-45
   benefits of diversity 242
   reliable varieties 240
   seeds, saving 242
   suppliers 244-5
Heptachlor 11
herbs 45, 174, 175, 179, 269-77
   annual 270, 271-2
   herb teams 275
   home-dried 116
   perennials 270, 273-4
   pots, in 146, 269
   trimming 276-7
   types 270-1
heritage vegetables *see* heirloom vegetables
Houdan **167**
humid temperate climate 260
Hyatt, Arthur 7

insecticides 17
insects 280-3 *see also* pest control
   predatory 283
ISA Browns 158, 160, **165**, 195

jams 120-1
jellies 120-1

kaffir lime 148, 251
kale 94
Klarkowski, Derryck 13

labelling
   name tags 51
   organic 19
ladybird beetles **286-7**
leaf miner **293**
leeks 90, 95, *98*, **219-20**
lemon grass 146, **206-7**
lemons 113-14
   dwarf 248-9
   'Eureka' 249, *250*
   'Lisbon' 250
   'Meyer' 250, *251*
lettuce **105**, 145, 151, 181, **220-1**
lime 17
limes **113-14**, 251
   dwarf 'Tahitian' *248*
   native 254
   'Tahiti' *251*
liquid food 94, 144, 147
location of garden 23-4
lucerne hay 125, 196

macadamias **264**
   dwarf 249
   Macadamia integrifolia 264
   Macadamia tetraphylla 264

Malay Game **169**
Maldison 10
mandarins 252
   dwarf 248
mangoes **264**
   dwarf 249
marigolds 153, 195
marjoram 179, 270, *274*, 275
marmalades 120-1
Mediterranean and inland climate 260
melons 146, **221**
mint 45, 179, 270, 273, 274, 275, *277*
mizuna **105**, **224**
Morus nigra 264
mulberries **265**
Murraya koenigii 179
mustard **105**, **224**

name tags, easy 51
nashi pears **265**
National Registration Authority for Agricultural and Veterinary Chemicals (NRAAVC) 11, 13
native animals 190
native plants 177, 191-2
nectarines, dwarf 249
nematodes 48, 195, 290
Nitrosol 182, 256

okra **222**
olive trees 175, **265**
onions 90, **108-9**, **223**
   white *98*
orange, dwarf 248-9
   'Valencia' 247, *248*
   'Washington Navel' *247*
oranges
   'Valencia' *250*
oregano 179, 273, 274, 275
organic gardening 17-19
   construction 23-32
   definition 17
organic labelling 19
Orpingtons **167**
overplanting 49

pak choy *see* Chinese chard
pansies 153
parsley 45, 97, 179, 270, 271, 275
parsnips 91, **106**, 146, 181, **224-5**
   'Hollow Crown' 240
passionfruit 147, 254-5
   growing **255**
   'Nellie Kelly' 255
paths 176, 190
paving stones 89
pea straw 125
peaches, dwarf 249
pears
   dwarf varieties 249

peas 88-9, **109**, 151, **225-6**
Pekin Bantam **166**
peppers, Liberty Bell *240*
permaculture 187-98
persimmons **265**
   dwarf 249
pest control 17, 280-94
pesticides 14, 194
pesto recipe 83, 117
Pestoil 182
pests 282
pets 157, 296
pickles 119
pineapples **266**
Pivot 13
plans *32*
   autumn planting *92-3*
   potager-style garden *178*
   spring planting *52-3*
planting
   autumn 85-99
   beans 47
   companion 195, 297
   fruit trees 257-8
   gluts, avoiding 37
   growth and care 54-61
   preparation 35-42
   quantity 37
   seedlings 36-7, 42
   seeds 36-7, 38-41
   shopping tips 36-7
   spring 45-61
   strawberry pots 50
   times 36
   tomatoes 46, 49
plants for children to grow 151
Polish **167**
pomelo 249
ponds 190-1
possums 97, **293-4**
potager-style gardens 175-85
potatoes 9, 99, **110**, 146, 151, 194, **226-7**
   pots, in 148
   Sapphire *9*
pots *see* containers
potting sheds 193-4
preserving 10, 118-21
   sterilising jars 121
pumpkin beetle **288**
pumpkins 61, **110-11**, 146, 151, **227-8**
   pumpkin and red lentil soup 80
pyrethrum 17

quinces **267**

radishes 7, **105**, **228-9**
rainbow chard *9*
rats **293-4**
recipes

   bread rolls with pesto and oven-dried tomatoes 83
   chocolate zucchini cake 69
   eggplant parmigiana 70
   pesto 83
   pumpkin and red lentil soup 80
   rhubarb and hazelnut tart 77
   strawberry and mint sorbet 73
   sultana carrot cheesecake 78
   tomato sauce 70
   tomatoes, oven-dried 83
   vegie patch salad 74
   zucchini relish 72
relishes 119
Rhode Island Reds 158, 160, 161
   Rhode Island Red Cross 160, **164**
Rhode Island Whites 158
rhubarb **115-16**, **229-30**
   rhubarb and hazelnut tart 77
rock phosphate 17
rocket **105**, *181*, **224**
root vegetables 91, 146
rosemary 45, 179, 270, *273*, *274*, *275*
Roundup 27

sage 45, 179, 270, *273*, *274*, *275*
salad greens 45, **105**, *181*, **224**
sandy soil 124-5
Savoy cabbage 145
scale insects **293**
scarecrow, making 63-7
scarlet runner beans *55*, *58*
Seale, Alan 10
Seasol 182, 194, 256
seedlings 36-7
   labelling 48
   planting 42, 47, 49
   spacing 89
   thinning out 56
   watering in 49
seeds 36-7
   broad beans 91
   carrots 91
   saving 242
   sowing 38-41, 47
shallots 90, **111**, 146, *180*, *181*, **230-1**
Silkies 161, **165**
silver beet 7, 95, **231-2**
Silver Spangled Hamburg **166**
site 23-4
size of beds 89
slugs **289-90**
small gardens 175-85
snails **289-90**
snow peas 88, *89*, *96*, **109**, *174*, *180*, *182*, **225-6**
soil 24-5, 187, 189
   clay 25
   clods 87
   compost *see* compost
   management 31-2

nematodes 48
organic mixes 24-5
preparing for seeds *38-9*
sowing seeds
containers, into 40
direct sowing 38
spinach *174*
English 181, **232**
spined citrus bugs 293
spring onions **111**, 146
spring planting 45-61
plan *52-3*
3 weeks after planting 54-5
4 weeks after planting 56-7
6 weeks after planting 58-9
11 weeks after planting 60
squash, button **104**
squash, summer *59, 60*
Standards Australia 13, 18, 144
Steiner, Rudolf 18
sticky traps 289
stink bugs **292**
stone fruits **266**
storage *see also* harvest and storage
ice-cube method 115
preserving 118-21
strawberries 45, 50, 151, 181, **256-7**
pots, in 50-1, *57, 59*, 148
strawberry and mint sorbet 73
subtropics 36, 259
Success 96
sugar snap peas 88, **109**, **225-6**
sultana carrot cheesecake 78
sun 23-4, 189
sunflowers 153
suppliers of heirloom/heritage plants 244-5
swedes 91
sweet corn *see* corn
sweet potato **233-4**
Swiss chard 95

tangelo
tarragon 179, 270, 276
tatsoi **205**
thyme 45, 179, 270, *273*, 274, 275
times for planting 36
tropics and subtropics 36
tomato sauce 70
tomatoes 8-9, 45, *55*, **116-17**, 181, 194, **234-5**
cocktail 45
Floradade *8*
green grape *9*
'Green Oxheart' *241*
'Grosse Lisse' 240
heirloom varieties *9*, 193-4
oven-dried 83
planting 49
pots, in 146
'Small Fry' 45

support 48
'Sweetie' 45
'Tiny Tim' 45
tripods 46
Transylvanian Naked Neck **167**
treated pine 30
trees 191
tripods for tomatoes 46
tropics 36, 259
turmeric **206-7**
turnips 91, *180, 181*, **236**

vacuum packing 121
vegetables
cool-season 35
gluts 37
heirloom 7-10, 192, 239-45
miniature 146
modern hybrids 240
root 91
warm-season 35
vegie patch salad 74

Wariapendi Nursery 191
warm-season vegetables 35
planting times 36
water tanks 196-7
watermelons **117**, 151
weeds 56, *57*
White Leghorn 160, 161, 195
White Leghorn Cross 160, **164**
whiteflies 289
wire mesh, galvanised 31, *32*
worm farms 135-7
Wyandotte Bantam **168**

Yates 13
Anti-Rot 42

Zero 27
zucchini 45, *54, 56, 60*, 61, **104**, 151, **237**
chocolate zucchini cake 69
relish 72

First published in Australia in 2009 by
Reed New Holland
An imprint of New Holland Publishers (Australia) Pty Ltd
Sydney • Auckland • London • Cape Town

1/66 Gibbes Street Chatswood NSW 2067 Australia
218 Lake Road Northcote Auckland New Zealand
86 Edgware Road London W2 2EA United Kingdom
80 McKenzie Street Cape Town 8001 South Africa

Copyright © 2009 New Holland Publishers (Australia) Pty Ltd
Copyright in text and images © 2009 Don Burke

All rights reserved. No part of this publication may be reproduced, stored in a retrieval system or transmitted, in any form or by any means, electronic, mechanical, photocopying, recording or otherwise, without the prior written permission of the publishers and copyright holders.

A record of this book is held at the National Library of Australia

ISBN 9781877069673

Publisher: Fiona Schultz
Publishing Manager: Lliane Clarke
Designer: Tania Gomes
Production Manager: Olga Dementiev
Printer: Toppan Leefung Printing Limited (China)

10 9 8 7 6 5 4 3 2

Author: Don Burke
Horticultural Consultant: Geoffrey Burnie
Editorial Consultant: Jamie McIlwraith
Production Coordinator: Chris Burke
Primary Photographer: Brent Wilson
Additional Photography: Jamie McIlwraith
Illustrations: Pamela Horsnell, Juno Creative Services
Design Consultant: Zora Regulic
Additional artwork: Kim Audsley, Ben Hewett & Maya Harrison

Photo credits:
Pages 164: White Leghorn Cross & 168 Araucana, by Andy Vardy
Page 247: Kath Kermode, Daley's Nursery
Page:176: Leigh Clapp
Pages 16, 294: Photolibrary

With thanks to: The wonderful Carah family, Nic Verzi, Der lieben Familie Napthali, Robyn Anderson, Megg Miller, Barter & Sons Hatchery, Rent-a-chook, Katie Marx, Brian Larkin, 'The Colonel' Bernie Gibson and my 'Pa', Arthur Hyatt who showed me how to grow vegies.

Plant		
Chicory	14-26	10-20
Chilli	20-22	12-14
Burke's Backyard Thai Chilli	16-20	*
Chinese broccoli	10-12	8
Chinese cabbage	10-12	8
Choko (sprouted fruit)	9-11	7-9
Cucumber	8-10	4-6
Eggplant	20-22	18-20
Endive	8-12	5-9
Herbs	14-16	4-6
Leeks	8-12	*
Lettuce (iceberg)	12-20	6-12
Combo/Salad Mix	8-12	4-12
Red Coral/Oak Leaf	8-11	4-6
Marrow/zucchini	6-10	4-6
Melon	8-14	5-10
Mustard	14-16	4
Onion	4-6	9-12
Onion (spring)	24-32	*
Parsnip	8-12	4-6
Pea (climbing)	18-20	16-24
Pea (dwarf)	14-16	15-17
Potato (tubers)	12-16	8-10
Pumpkin	#	6-8
Radish	14-16	16-20
Rhubarb (seed)	6-8	10-12
Rhubarb (crowns)	16-20	4-6
Salsify	#	6-10
Senposai	20-22	8-12
Shallot (bulbs)	4-5	*
Silver beet	#	12-14
Spinach	8-12	4-6
Squash	8-10	4-5
Sweet corn	12-14	8-10
Sweet potato (shoots)	12-16	9-12
Tomato	#	18-20
Turnip	12-20	8-12
	10-12	6-10

not usually grown from seed by home gardeners * not widely available as a seedling (grow from seed)

Organic Planting Calendar

This handy chart shows you when to plant and sow vegetables Australia-wide and when you can expect to harvest them.

CLIMATIC ZONES

- ▬ tropical/subtropical
- ▬ temperate
- ▬ cold

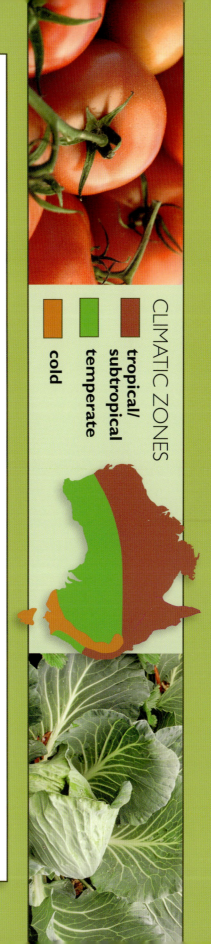

BEST MONTHS TO SOW SEED

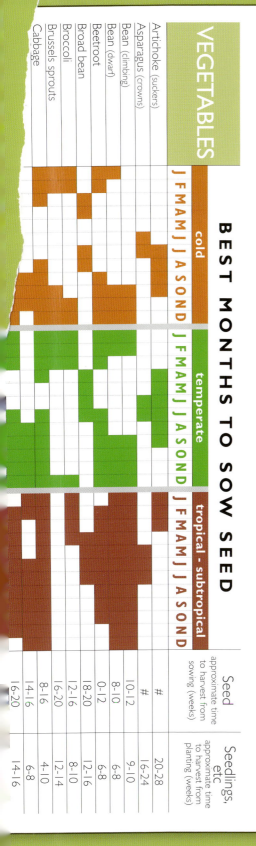

VEGETABLES	cold / temperate / tropical-subtropical (J F M A M J J A S O N D)	Seed — approximate time to harvest from sowing (weeks)	Seedlings, etc — approximate time to harvest from planting (weeks)
Artichoke (suckers)		#	20-28
Asparagus (crowns)		#	16-24
Bean (climbing)		10-12	9-10
Bean (dwarf)		8-10	6-8
Beetroot		10-12	6-8
Broad bean		18-20	12-16
Broccoli		12-16	8-10
Brussels sprouts		16-20	12-14
Cabbage		8-16	4-10
		14-16	6-8
		16-20	14-16